Science

with **Chapter-wise Previous 10 Year** (2013 - 2022) Questions

DISHA Publications Inc.

45, 2nd Floor, Maharishi Dayanand Marg,
Corner Market, Malviya Nagar, new Delhi -110017
Tel: 49842349/ 49842350

Typeset By

DISHA DTP Team

Preface

We are pleased to launch the thoroughly revised 4th edition of **Olympiad Champs Science Class 1** which is the first of its kind book on Olympiad in many ways.

The Unique Selling Proposition of this new edition is the inclusion of past year questions till 2022 of different Olympiad exams held in schools.

The book is aimed at achieving not only success but deep rooted learning in children. It is prepared on content based on National Curriculum Framework prescribed by NCERT. All the text books, syllabi and teaching practices within the education programme in India must follow NCF. Hence, Olympiad Champs become an ideal book not only for the Olympiad Exams but also for strengthening the concepts for Class 1

There is an exhaustive range of thought provoking questions in MCQ format to test the student's knowledge thoroughly. The questions are designed so as to test the knowledge, comprehension, evaluation, analytical and application skills. Solutions and explanations are provided for all questions. The questions are divided into two levels-Level 1 and Level 2. The first level, Level 1, is the beginner's level which comprises of questions like fillers, analogy and odd one out. When the children covers Level 1, it means his basic knowledge about the subject is clear and now he is ready for Level 2. The second level is the advanced level. Level 2 comprises of techniques like matching, chronological sequencing, picture, passage and feature based, statement correct/ incorrect, integer based, puzzle, grid based, crossword, venn diagram, table/ chart based and much more.

The first concern which each parent faces is how to make their children read a book especially when it is based on academics. Keeping this in mind interesting facts, real life examples, historical preview, short cuts to problem solving, charts, diagrams, illustrations and poems are added.

With the vision to remove all the misconception a child may have pertaining to the subject, to relate his knowledge to the real world and to develop a deeper understanding of the subject, this book will cater all the requirements of the students who are going to appear in Olympiads.

While preparing this book, some errors might have crept in. We request our readers to identify those errors and send it across on **feedback_disha@aiets.co.in.**

We wish you all the best for your Olympiads and happy reading.......

Team Disha

For feedback : feedback_disha@aiets.co.in.

CONTENTS

1 CHAPTER FOREWORD

Have you seen your book moving from your bag to your friend's bag? Did your pencil walk out of the pencil-box? There are some things that are living while some things are non-living.

Look at the pictures given below and tick (✓) for the things that are living.

When you finish reading this chapter, you will know more ways to identify if a thing is living or not.

1 Chapter

Living and Non-living Things

Real life examples

- A teddy bear cannot grow so it is a non-living thing.
- A car cannot move on its own so it is a non-living thing.

LEARNING OBJECTIVES

This lesson will help you to:

- Study about living and non-living things.
- Learn the features of living and non-living things.
- Differentiate between living and non-living things.

INTRODUCTION

Have you noticed the different things around you. For example tables, chairs, toys, plants, birds etc.

Some of these things can grow in size but some can not. For Example: Plants can grow but toys can't. They have the same size throughout the life. This is because plants are **living** and toys are **non-living things.**

LIVING AND NON LIVING THINGS

Living Things: The things which possess life and have the ability to feel, grow, breath, reproduce, response and grow are called living thing.

They are capable of responding to stimuli or evolve and adapt to their environment. For example Humans, Animals & Plants.

Non-Living Things: Non-living things are the one which has stopped displaying or don't show the characteristics of life.

Thus, they lack or no longer displaying or don't show the capability for growth, reproduction, respiration and movement. They also are not capable of responding to stimuli or evolve and adapt to their environment.

DIFFERENCE BETWEEN LIVING AND NON-LIVING THINGS

Living things are different from non-living things in the following ways:

1. **Food:** All living things need food to carry out all the activities.

Plants make their own food in the presence of water, sunlight and soil. Animals and human beings depend on plants for food.

Non-living things do not need food for their survival.

2. **Growth:** All living things follow a life cycle in which they are born, grow and finally die.

A seed grows into a seedling, then into a plant and finally into a tree. A baby grows into an adult and finally becomes old. Animals also grow from babies to adults.

As the living beings grow, they change in size, shape and appearance.

Non-living things do not grow and they remain the same.

3. **Movement:** All living things move from one place to another. Animals move in search of food. Some animals hunt for their food while others graze on grass. Birds fly in the air. Human beings roam for different activities. Plants though living do not move from place to place. They are held in the soil by their roots. Certain plants can move their parts like leaves which open and chose at night and branches of a sunflower always bend in the direction of sunlight.

We need to push or pull to move a **non-living thing**. Non-living things cannot move on their own.

4. **Breathe:** All living things also need to breathe and stay alive. All living things have an organ which helps in breathing. Human beings and many animals breathe through nose. Insects have tiny air holes in their body called as spiracles. Fish breathe through gills. Plants breathe through openings, called stomata, on their leaves.

Non-living things do not have life, they do not breathe.

Try this

- Keep your teddy bear and a plant in the flower pot in your drawing room. After a week what will you notice? The teddy bear will remain same in size whereas the plant will grow in size. Do you know the reason behind this?

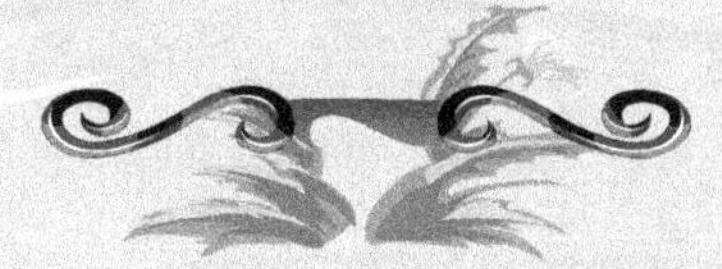

5. **Reproduction:** All living things produce more of its kind by the process of reproduction. Some animals lay eggs while others including human beings give birth to young ones. Seeds produce plants.

Non-living things do not reproduce.

6. **Response:** Living things have sense organs (eyes, nose, tongue, skin and ears) due to which they respond to changes in their environment. Animals also feel and respond to changes in their environment. Bears hibernate in winters to protect itself from cold. Dogs have sharp sense of smell. Plants do not grow in the absence of light, water and air.

Non-living things do not feel. They are not affected by any changes around them.

Living Things	Non-living Things

	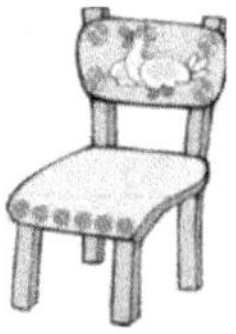
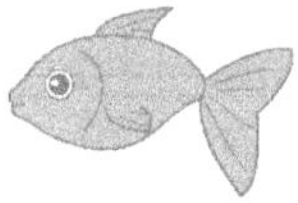	

	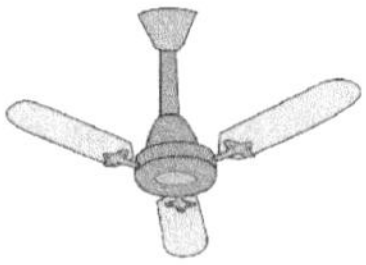

Do You Know?

❖ There is a basic structural and functional unit inside all the living organisms called **cell**. This unit performs couple of activities inside to help the organisms.

Multiple Choice Questions

LEVEL 1

1. Choose the living thing from the pictures shown below.

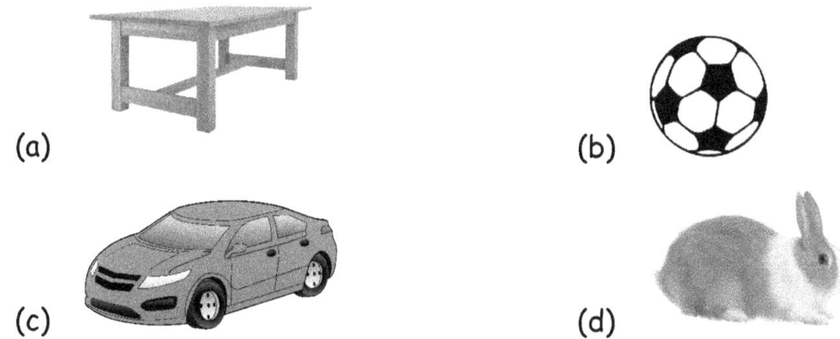

(a) (b)

(c) (d)

2. Choose the Non-living thing from the pictures shown below.

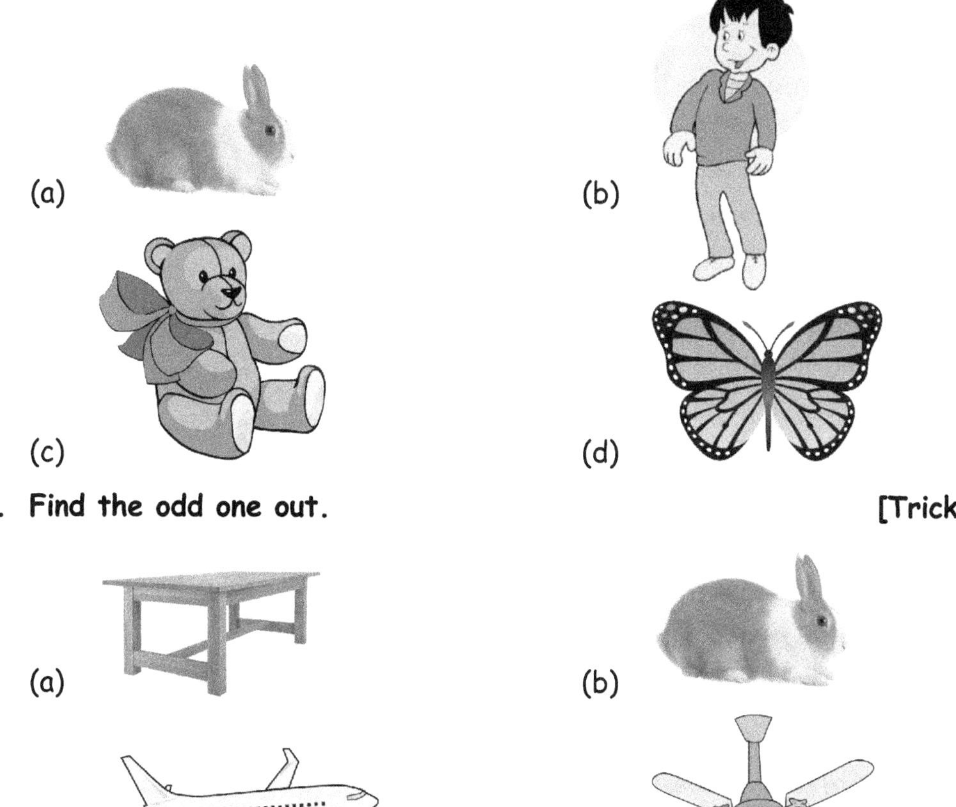

(a) (b)

(c) (d)

3. Find the odd one out. [Tricky]

(a) (b)

(c) (d)

4. **Which of the following is/are the characteristic features of all living things? [2013]**
   (a) Living things need food. (b) Living things need air.
   (c) Living things need water. (d) All of the above.
5. **All living things can ________ from one place to the other.**
   (a) Water (b) Non-living (c) Air (d) Move
6. **A chair cannot move as it is a ________ thing.**
   (a) Water (b) Non-living (c) Air (d) Move
7. **The two major categories in which all the things can be categorized are. [Tricky]**
   (a) Living things and non-living things (b) Table and chair
   (c) Tools and machines (d) Apple and banana
8. **Living things cannot live without ________. [Tricky]**
   (a) air (b) fan
   (c) phone (d) none of these
9. **Which of the following things remain same in size after many years?**
   (a) Plants (b) Fish (c) Teddy Bear (d) Dog
10. **Which of the following is correct about living things? [2014]**
    (a) Living things need food to grow.
    (b) Living things remain the same in size.
    (c) Living things cannot eat.
    (d) All of these
11. **Living things will die if they do not get ________. [Tricky]**
    1. Air 2. Water 3. Food
    (a) 1 only (b) 1 and 2 only
    (c) 1 and 3 only (d) 1, 2 and 3
12. **How are living things different from non-living? [Tricky]**
    (a) Living things are tall. Non-living things are short.
    (b) Living things are young. Non-living things are old.
    (c) Living things need food, water and air. Non-living things do not.
    (d) Living things do not make noise. Non-living things make noise.
13. **Which one of the following is a true statement? [Tricky]**
    (a) Cow is a non living thing (b) Rabbit is a non living thing
    (c) Elephant is a living thing (d) Cat is a non living thing

14. **Which one of the following is a/an non-living thing?**
    (a) Dog (b) Cow (c) Elephant (d) Pencil

15. **Which of the following statements suggest that a battery-operated car is NOT a living thing? [2016, Tricky]**
    1. It takes up space.
    2. It is hard and shiny.
    3. It does not reproduce.
    4. It does not move on its own.

    (a) 1 and 2 only (b) 1 and 3 only (c) 2 and 4 only (d) 3 and 4 only

DIRECTIONS (Qs. 16 to 17) : The diagram below shows four hamsters kept in four different containers. They were left untouched for two weeks. Study the diagram and answer the questions. [Critical Thinking]

16. **Which hamster is likely to live for the longest time?**
    (a) 1 (b) 2 (c) 3 (d) 4

17. **Which hamster is likely to live for the shortest time?**
    (a) 1 (b) 2 (c) 3 (d) 4

18. **Refer to the given experiment. Cockroach 1 died before cockroach 2. What was the most likely reason? [Critical Thinking]**

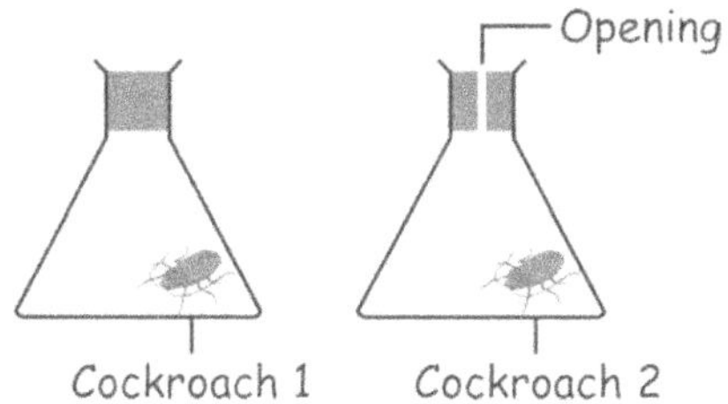

    (a) It did not get air (b) It did not have food.
    (c) It did not have water. (d) It did not have food and water.

19. Study the table given below carefully. **[2016, Tricky]**

Group A	Group B
Rose	Toy car
Butterfly	Aeroplane
Orchid	Remote control

Which of the following shows suitable headings for the groups?

	Group A	**Group B**
(a)	Non-living things	Living things
(b)	Plants	Animals
(c)	Living things	Non-living things
(d)	Flowers	Fruits

20. Some features of living things are given in the box. **[2017, Tricky]**

1. Can grow in size.
2. Can breathe.
3. Can move from one place to another on their own.
4. Can feel.

Which of these features are NOT found only in all living things?

(a) 1, 2 and 3 only (b) 1 and 3 only

(c) 1, 3 and 4 only (d) 2 and 4 only

21. Plants are living, but they CANNOT _____ like animals. **[2015]**

(a) Breathe (b) Reproduce

(c) Grow (d) Change position

22. ________ things can ________. **(2019)**

(a) Natural reproduce (b) Man-made, grow

(c) Living, reproduce (d) Non-living, feel

23. Which of the following comes from a living thing? **(2019)**

(a)  (b)  (c)  (d)

24. Which of the following statements is correct? **(2020)**

(a) All living things are natural.

(b) All non-living things are man-made

(c) All living things can move from one place to another.

(d) All non-living things can grow and increase in size.

25. **Refer to the given diagram and select the option that correctly identifies X.** **(2021)**

(a) Eraser
(b) Butterfly
(c) Tree
(d) Water

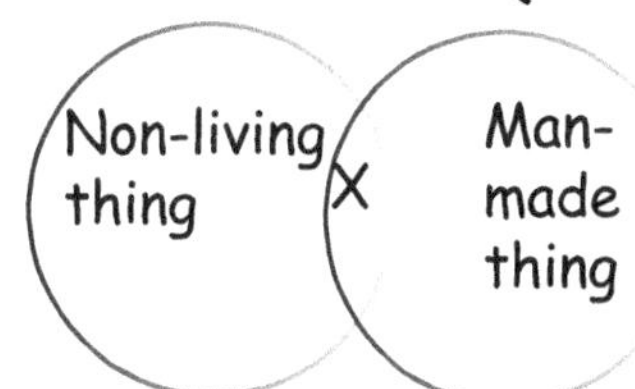

26. **Names of how many man-made things are there in the given word grid?** **(2021)**

A	B	D	A	I	R
C	U	P	G	R	H
F	J	K	M	I	I
O	C	O	I	N	Q
L	Q	E	E	G	P
W	A	T	E	R	N

(a) 3 (b) 4 (c) 5 (d) 6

27. **The given picture shows that living thing X, _____.** **(2022)**

(a) Needs water to live
(b) Can breathe
(c) Can feel
(d) Reproduces

28. **Select the odd one out among the following.** **(2022)**

(b) 

(d) 

29. **Select the option that pairs one living thing and one non-living thing correctly.** **(2022)**

(a) Mug, Sun
(b) Frog, Chair
(c) Sunflower paint, Butterfly
(d) Both a and c

30. Which one of the following does not eat food and also never feels hungry? **(2022)**

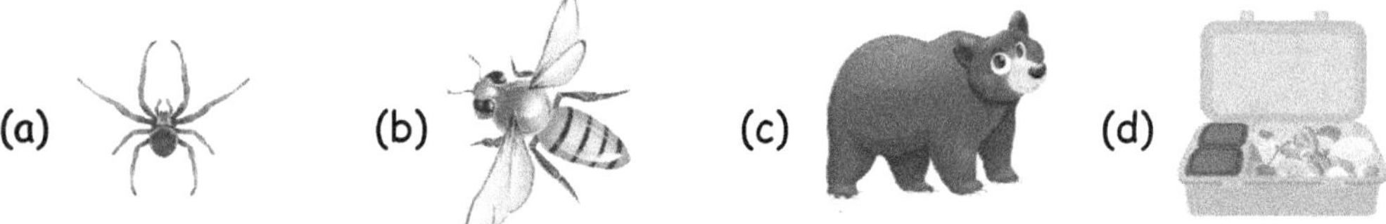

(a) (b) (c) (d)

31. Identify the living things in the figure shown below. **(2022)**

(a) 1, 3 and 4 (b) 1, 2 and 3 (c) 5 and 6 (d) 3, 4 and 6

LEVEL 2

1. **Which one is a characteristic of non-living thing?**
   (a) Non-living things do not grow.
   (b) Non-living things can move from place to place
   (c) Non-living things need food to live
   (d) None of the above
2. **Match the column (I) with column (II).** **[Tricky]**

Column I		Column II	
A.	Aeroplane	1.	Air, Water & Food
B.	Non-living thing	2.	Non-living thing
C.	Living thing needs	3.	Table

	A	B	C
(a)	3	2	1
(b)	2	1	3
(c)	2	3	1
(d)	1	2	3

3. **Teacher gave a list to Lata and asked her to write example of the things whose characters were mentioned in the list. [2016]**
   The list completed by Lata is shown below.
   1. Thing that can breathe, grow and reproduce - Ant
   2. Non- living thing that can increase in size - Gel bead
   3. Living thing that connot move - Snail
   4. Thing that cannot breathe and reproduce but can move - Car

   Which of the entries made by Lata are correct?
   (a) 1, 2 and 3 only (b) 1, 2 and 4 only
   (c) 2, 3 and 4 only (d) 2 and 4 only

4. **Consider the following statement and choose the correct answers.**
   Statement A : Table can move so it is a living thing. **[Critical Thinking]**
   Statement B : A plant is a living thing because it can grow.
   (a) Statement 'A' is true and Statement 'B' is false.
   (b) Statement 'B' is true and Statement 'A' is false.
   (c) Both the statement are true.
   (d) Both the statements are false.

5. **Identify 'X' and 'Y'. [Tricky]**

Living thing	'X'	Plant
Non-living thing	Aeroplane	'Y'

   (a) X = Television, Y = Toy (b) X = Cat, Y = Cow
   (c) X = Cat, Y = Table (d) X = Cow, Y = Plant

6. **Which of the following groups refers only to non-living things?**
   (a) Table, Aeroplane, Plants (b) Teddy bear, Chair, Fan
   (c) Plant, Cow, Aeroplane (d) Birds, Plants, Cat

7. **Study the given table carefully. Which of the following can be placed at P and Q ? [2015]**

Group 1	Group 2
Rose	Toy car
P	Razor
Orchid	Q

	P	Q
(a)	Butterfly	Chair
(b)	Chair	Butterfly
(c)	Banana plant	Dog
(d)	Dog	Banana plant

8. **Which of the following is true?**
   (a) Plants are non-living things.
   (b) Plants do not grow.
   (c) All living things can grow on their own.
   (d) A toy can move from place to place with its own.

9. **Which of the following does NOT show a living thing responding to its environment?** **[2014]**
   (a) A rat running away when being chased.
   (b) A door closing when it is blown by the wind.
   (c) A tortoise going back into its shell when it is touched.
   (d) None of these

10. **Which of the following word is given wrong under the heading in the following table?** **[Tricky]**

Living things	Non-living things
Table	Aeroplane
Birds	Chair
Plant	Teddy bear
Rabbit	Pencil

   (a) Rabbit (b) Table (c) Pencil (d) Plant

11. **Book, flowers, cars, aeroplane, plant, table, chair, birds.** **[Tricky]**
   From the above list, identify the non-living things.
   (a) Birds, Flower, Table, Book, Car (b) Plants, Flowers, Aeroplane, Car, Book
   (c) Table, Chair, Aeroplane, Book, Car (d) Flowers, Chair, Birds, Table, Plant

12. **How many number of living things are present in the box?**

Rabbit	Cow	Table	Sofa
Television	Plant	Birds	Fish

   (a) 2 (b) 3 (c) 5 (d) 6

13. **Read the sentence carefully and find True (T) and False (F).** **[Tricky]**
   1. Living things need air, water and food to grow.
   2. Plants are living things and aeroplane is a non-living thing.
   3. A chair can move by its own, it is a living thing.

   (a) TFT (b) TTT (c) TTF (d) FTF

14. **Is car a living thing?** **[2014]**
   (a) Yes, a car can move on its own.
   (b) No, it cann't grow in size.
   (c) Some cars are living things and some are non-living things.
   (d) None of these

15. Which of the following is TRUE? [Tricky]

(a) Plants are non-living things.

(b) All living things can grow on their own.

(c) Living thing needs air, water & food to live.

(d) Both (b) and (c)

16. Categorise the items into living and non-living and count the number of each. Boy, chair, fish, toy, butterfly, helicopter. [Tricky]

(a) Living things - 2, Non-living things - 4

(b) Living-things - 3, Non-living things - 3

(c) Living-things - 4, Non-living things - 2

(d) Living-things - 5, Non-living things - 1

17. All living things cannot stay alive and will die within minutes in the absence of ____________.

(a) Food (b) Light (c) Air (d) Water

18. Ravi planted so many plants in his garden but never gave water to them. As a result the plant couldn't grow. Ravi started crying. How will you help Ravi?

(a) Tell him to keep the plants in the dark room.

(b) Tell him to give water the plant daily.

(c) Tell him to give fruits & vegetables to plant.

(d) Both (b) and (c)

19. A rabbit was kept in a closed box with food and water, yet it died. Which of the following could be a reason for this? [Tricky]

(a) The rabbit did not get air

(b) The rabbit did not move

(c) The rabbit did not get enough space

(d) All of these

20. Which of the following statements is correct? [Tricky]

(a) Air is a living thing because it can move.

(b) Banyan tree is a non-living thing because it cannot move.

(c) A balloon is a living thing because it grows in size when air is pumped into it.

(d) A wheat grain is a living thing because it can grow into a new plant.

Direction (Qs. 21 to 23): Read the passage carefully and answer the question. [Critical Thinking]

There are so many things which remain same in size after so many years because they are non-living things. For example pencil, table, toys etc. You can walk, run, move from one place to another, birds, butterfly and fishes can also move on their own because they are living things.

21. **Which of the following is a living thing?**
    (a) Pencil (b) Birds
    (c) Boy (d) both (b) and (c)
22. **Which of the following can grow in size?**
    (a) Aeroplane (b) Birds (c) Table (d) Chair
23. **Which of the following can move from one place to another on its own?**
    (a) Toy (b) table (c) Fish (d) Pencil
24. **Study the given picture. What does it show?**

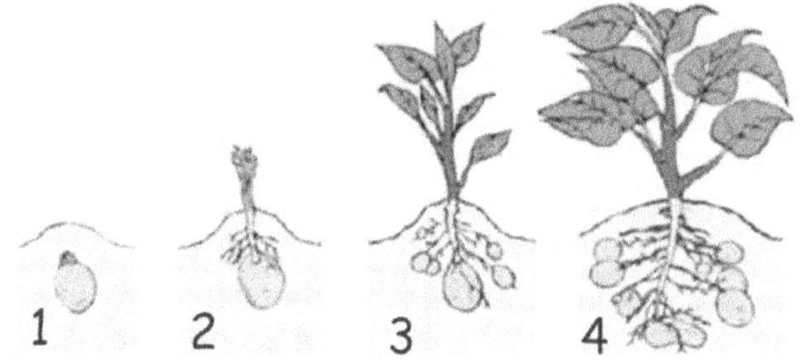

(a) Living things can grow (b) Living things can move
(c) Living things need food (d) All of these

25. **Look at the classification table given below.** **[Critical Thinking]**

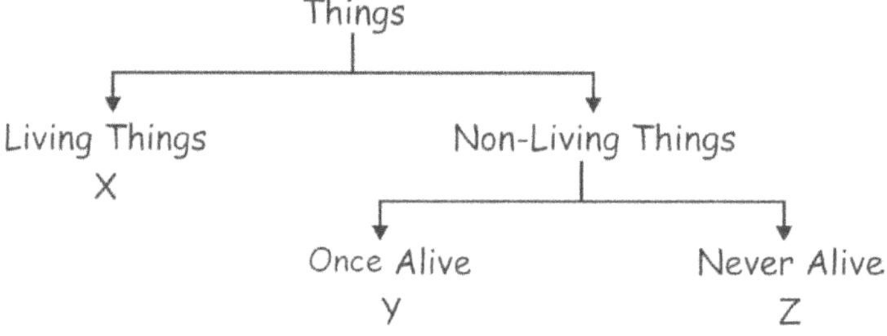

Which of the following represents 'X', 'Y' and 'Z' correctly?

	X	Y	Z
(a)	Orchid	Steel ruler	Plastic Spoon
(b)	Seed	Paper cup	Wooden chair
(c)	Flour	Dolphin	Stone
(d)	Lizard	Wooden chair	Rock

26. **Living things reproduce so that _____________.** **[2015, Tricky]**
    (a) They cannot be eaten up by other living organisms
    (b) There will always be living things of their own kind
    (c) They can occupy a large space
    (d) They will not have to fight for food

27. All living things need _____________ to stay alive.

1. Air 2. Sunlight 3. Food 4. Water

(a) 1 and 2 only (b) 1, 3 and 4

(c) 1, 2 and 3 only (d) 1, 2, 3 and 4

28. Which of the following statements is INCORRECT? [Tricky]

(a) Non-living things can move by themselves.

(b) Some living things can make their own food.

(c) Living things can move by themselves.

(d) Plans do not move from one place to another.

29. Study the given chart carefully. [Critical Thinking]

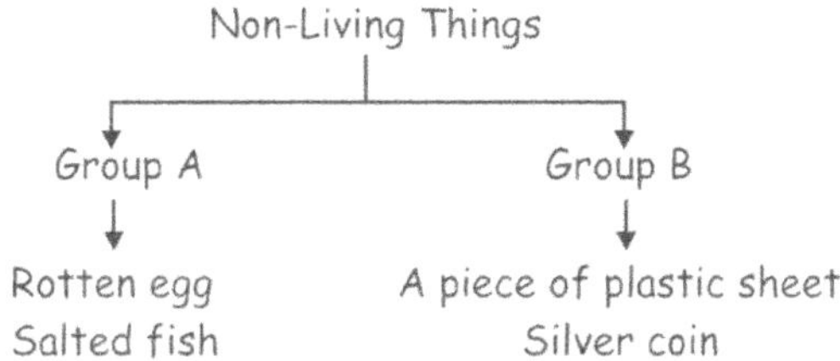

Which of the following can be classified under Group A?

(a) A plastic toy (b) Newspapers

(c) A crawling snail (d) A metal blade

30. Each of the following observations tells us what living things can do. Which of the following have been WRONGLY paired? [2016,Tricky]

	Observations	Living things can
1.	A rabbit gives birth.	Grow
2.	A caterpillar turns into pupa and then a butterfly.	Reproduce
3.	A bee flies from one flower to another.	Move
4.	A leaf withers and turns down.	Die

(a) 1 only (b) 1 and 2 only

(c) 1 and 4 only (d) 1, 3 and 4 only

31. The picture below shows a boy playing with a ball. [Tricky]

Which of the following statements is true regarding this?

(a) Both the ball and the boy can move on their own.

(b) Both the boy and the ball cannot move on their own.

(c) The ball can move on its own while the boy cannot.

(d) The boy can move on his own while the ball cannot.

32. Manya notices that the Venus flytrap plant captures insects by shutting its two leaves like a shell when an insect lands on them. This shows us that living things ___________. **[2017, Tricky]**

1. Can grow
2. Can reproduce
3. Respond to touch
4. Can move by themselves

(a) 1 and 2 only (b) 2 and 4 only (c) 3 and 4 only (d) 1, 2, 3 and 4

Direction (Qs. 33 to 37): Fill in the blanks in the passage given below.

[Critical Thinking]

Living things are those which can _______(33) _______ on its own. For example _______(34)______. They need food, air and _______(35) _______ to live and grow. Non-living things cannot grow. They remain of _______(36) _______ size. A _______(37) _______ cannot grow after many years.

33. (a) grow (b) size (c) tall (d) None of these

34. (a) Table (b) Plant (c) Aeroplane (d) Water

35. (a) Stone (b) Plant (c) Water (d) Books

36. (a) same (b) big (c) small (d) none of these

37. (a) living (b) non-living (c) both (a) and (b) (d) none of these

38. Mala kept two rabbits under different conditions as shown below.

[Critical Thinking]

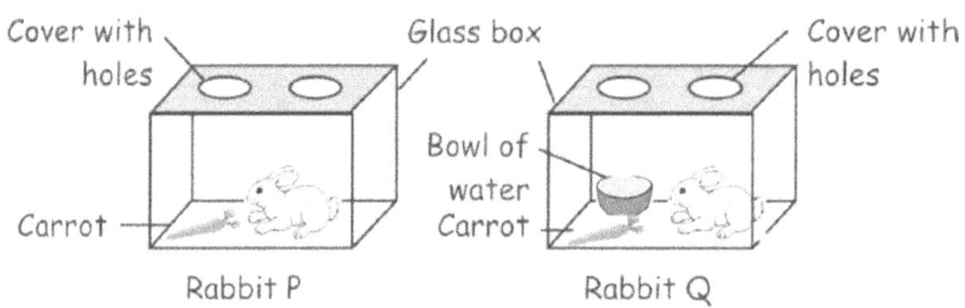

Which rabbit will NOT survive after one week?

(a) Rabbit P, because it did not get air.

(b) Rabbit Q, because it did not get air.

(c) Rabbit P, because it did not get water.

(d) Rabbit Q, because it could not move about.

39. Which of the following is correct?

(a) Computer is a living thing (b) Television is a living thing

(c) Bird is a living thing (d) Basket is a living thing

40. Which of the following show the characteristics of a living thing? **(2018)**

1. A football decreases in size when deflated.
2. A caterpillar turns into pupa.
3. A flower grows into fruit
4. A ship moves in water.

(a) 1 and 4 only (b) 1 and 3 only (c) 2 and 3 only (d) 2 and 4 only

41. Sushant has made the following table about characteristics of living and non-living things, but he made a mistake. Identify the mistake and select the correct option. (2020)

	Characteristics	Living things	Non-living things
P.	Breath	Yes	No
Q.	Feel	Yes	No
R.	Reproduce	No	Yes
S.	Grow	Yes	No

(a) P (b) Q (c) R (d) S

42. Read the given sentence. (2020)

Aditya wore a sweater when he tell cold.

The sentence indicates that living things _____.

(a) Grow and die (b) Reproduce

(c) Can feel (d) Need air, food and water

43. Siya paired one living thing and one non-living thing together but in doing so she made an incorrect pair. (2020)

Select the incorrect paW.

(a) Bird - Mountain (b) Fish - Clock

(c) Rose plant - Cycle (d) River - Book

44. Which of the following statement(s) is/are correct? (2021)

1. A dancing doll is a living thing as it can move its body parts.
2. Grapevine is a non-living thing as it cannot move or make sound.
3. Fish is a living thing as it can feel.
4. All man-made things are made from things that were once alive.

(a) 1 and 2 only (b) 3 only (c) 1, 2 and 4 only (d) 1 and 3 only

RESPONSE GRID

LEVEL 1

1. a b c d	2. a b c d	3. a b c d	4. a b c d	5. a b c d
6. a b c d	7. a b c d	8. a b c d	9. a b c d	10. a b c d
11. a b c d	12. a b c d	13. a b c d	14. a b c d	15. a b c d
16. a b c d	17. a b c d	18. a b c d	19. a b c d	20. a b c d
21. a b c d	22. a b c d	23. a b c d	24. a b c d	25. a b c d
26. a b c d	27. a b c d	28. a b c d	29. a b c d	30. a b c d
31. a b c d				

LEVEL 2

1. a b c d	2. a b c d	3. a b c d	4. a b c d	5. a b c d
6. a b c d	7. a b c d	8. a b c d	9. a b c d	10. a b c d
11. a b c d	12. a b c d	13. a b c d	14. a b c d	15. a b c d
16. a b c d	17. a b c d	18. a b c d	19. a b c d	20. a b c d
21. a b c d	22. a b c d	23. a b c d	24. a b c d	25. a b c d
26. a b c d	27. a b c d	28. a b c d	29. a b c d	30. a b c d
31. a b c d	32. a b c d	33. a b c d	34. a b c d	35. a b c d
36. a b c d	37. a b c d	38. a b c d	39. a b c d	40. a b c d
41. a b c d	42. a b c d	43. a b c d	44. a b c d	

Solutions with Explanation

LEVEL 1

1. **(d)** Rabbit is an animal which is a living thing.
2. **(c)** Teddy bear is a non-living thing.
3. **(b)** Rabbit is a living thing and other three (table, aeroplane and fan) are non-living.
4. **(d)** Living thing needs air, water and food.

5. (d) All living things can move from one place to the other.

6. (b) A chair cannot move, as it is a non-living thing.

7. (a) The two major categories in which all the things can be categorised are living and non-living things.

8. (a) cannot live without air.

9. (c) A teddy bear is a non-living thing which never grows and remains the same in size.

10. (a) Living things need food to grow.

11. (d) Living things will die if they do not get air, water and food.

12. (c) Living things need food, water and air but non-living things do not.

13. (c) 14. (d) 15. (d) 16. (b) 17. (a) 18. (a) 19. (c)

20. (a)

21. (d) Plants are living but they cannot change their position, as they cannot move from one place place to another.

22. (c) Living things can reproduce.

23. (b) We get wood from plants which are living things.

24. (a)

25. (a) Eraser is a non-living thing that made by a man.

26. (a) (3) Cup, Coin and Ring are man made things.

27. (a) X is a plant and it needs water to live.

28. (c) Bird is a living thing. All others are non-living things.

29. (b) Frog is a living thing and chair is a non-living thing.

30. (d) Non living things does not eat food and also never feels hungry.

31. (b) All are living thing except first in box.

LEVEL 2

1. (a) Non-living things do not grow.

2. (c) Aeroplane is a non-living thing, table is an example of non-living things. Living things need air, water & food to grow.

3. (b) Snail is a living thing that can move.

4. (b) Statement 'B' is true, plant is a living thing Statement 'A' is false because table is a non-living thing so it cannot move.

5. (c) 'X' is cat which is a living thing .'Y' is table which is a non-living thing.

6. (b) Teddy bear, chair and fan are non-living things.

7. (a) Group 1 shows the list of living things and group 2 shows the list of non-living things. So, butterfly can be placed in group 1 and chair in the group 2.
8. (c) All living things can grow on their own.
9. (b)
10. (b) Table, because it is a non-living thing.
11. (c) Table, chair, aeroplane, book and car are non-living things.
12. (c) Rabbit, cow, plant, birds, fish
13. (c) A chair cannot move as it is a non-living thing.
14. (b) Car is not a living thing because it cannot grow in size.
15. (d) All living things can grow on their own & need air, water and food to live.
16. (b) Living thing - 3 (Boy, fish, butterfly). Non-living thing = 3 (Chair, Toy, helicopter).
17. (c)
18. (b) Plants being a living thing need water to grow.
19. (a) 20. (d)
21. (d) Boy and bird both are living things.
22. (b) Birds can grow in size.
23. (c) Fish can move from one place to another on its own.

24. (a)	25. (d)	26. (b)
27. (d)	28. (a)	29. (b)
30. (b)	31. (d)	32. (c)
33. (a) grow	34. (b) Plant	35. (c) Water
36. (a) same	37. (b) non-living	38. (c)

39. (c)
40. (c) A flower grows into fruit and a caterpillar turns into pupa.
41. (c) 42. (c) 43. (d)
44. (b) Fish is a living thing as it can feel.

2 CHAPTER FOREWORD

Did you see that pretty little rose plant that grows in your garden? Did you notice that long tree in the park where you go to play?

All these are types of plants that grow differently in different places.

Name three plants that you eat.

1. ______________________________

2. ______________________________

3. ______________________________

Name four flowers that smell good.

1. ______________________________

2. ______________________________

3. ______________________________

4. ______________________________

When you finish reading this chapter, you will be able to tell names of more flowers, plants, trees etc. You will also know more about the world of plants.

Chapter 2

Plants

LEARNING OBJECTIVES

This lesson will help you to:

- Gain knowledge about plants.
- Learn about different parts of a plant.
- Study different types of plants.
- Know about the various food items obtained from plants.

INTRODUCTION

Have you noticed your green friends on the way while coming to school, on the road side, in the garden and in the park.

These are the plants which give us clean and fresh air. Let us study more about plants:

Plants : Plants are green in colour. They gives us sweet fruits, vegetables and beautiful flowers.

For example :

Rose plant

Money plant

PARTS OF PLANT

Plants consist of different parts. Each of the part plays a very important role:

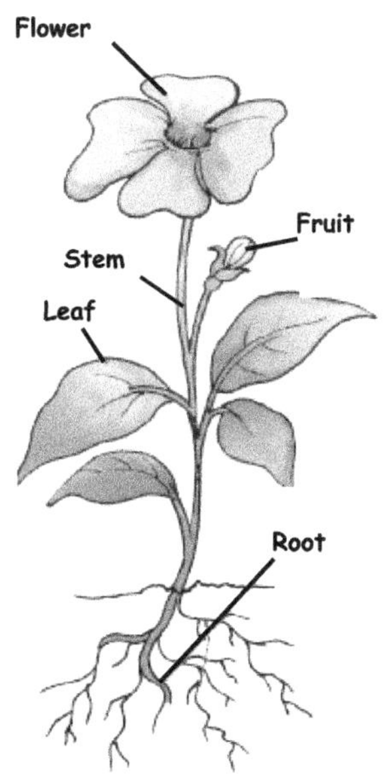

The different parts of a plant are: Root, Stem, leaves, flower and fruit.

(1) **Roots:** Roots are the lowest part of a plant that grow inside the surface of soil. They hold the plant in the soil.

(2) **Stem:** Stem is the part of plant which grows above the surface of soil. It bears leaf, flower and fruit. Stem provides support to the upper part of the plant. It also carried foods & water to every part of plant.

(3) **Leaves:** Leaves are the green part of a plant where food is made. Leaves are of different shapes, sizes and colours.

Real Life Connect

❖ Commonly found flowers.

Rose **Marigold**

❖ Commonly used vegetables.

Potato **Brinjal**

❖ Commonly used fruits.

Mango **Apple**

(4) **Flower:** Flowers are the most colourful part of a plant. Flowers are of different shapes, sizes and colours. Flower changes into fruit.

(5) **Fruit:** Fruit is the fleshy and eatable part of a plant.

For example: Apple, Mango, Water-melon.

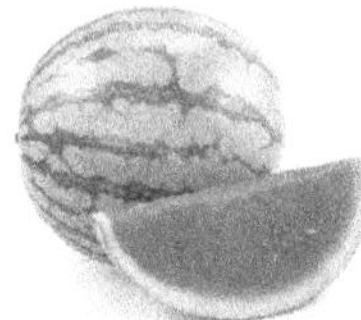

Fruits contain seeds. Some fruits like Mango have one seed. Papaya and Water-melon have many seeds. Seeds give rise to a new plant.

Mango Seed

Papaya Seeds

TYPES OF PLANTS

You might have noticed that some plants are very big and some are small and some are very small.

On the basis of size, plants can be of 3 different types: Herbs, Shrubs and Trees.

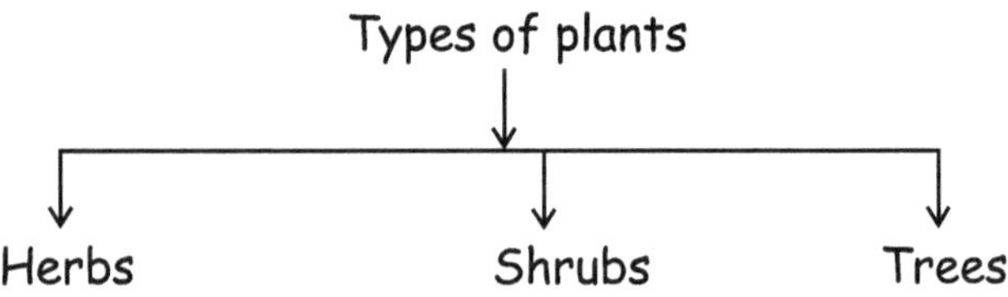

Herbs: Herbs are very small plants with soft stem.

For example : Coriander, Grass, etc.

Amazing Facts

- The world's largest flower is ***Rafflesia arnoldi.*** It can grow to the size of an umbrella.

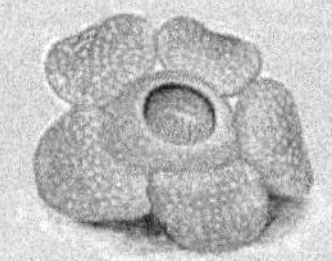

Rafflesia arnoldi

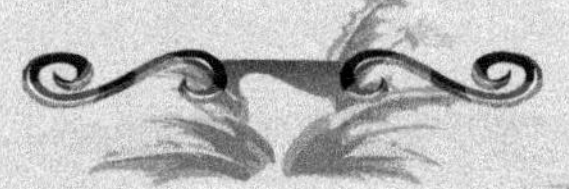

Misconcept /Concept

- **Misconcept:** Tomato is a vegetable.

  Concept: Tomato is NOT a vegetable, it is a fruit as it contains seeds. It can be consumed in different ways as raw, in salad, sauces, juices etc.
- **Misconcept:** Cauliflower is a vegetable.

  Concept: Cauliflower is actually an immature flower head. This flower is used as vegetable.

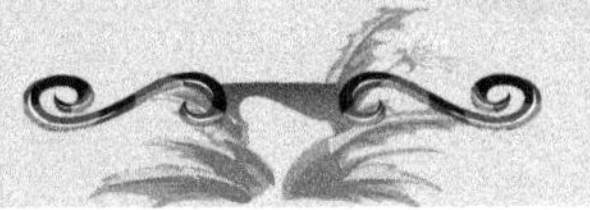

Do you Know

- Tulsi is an important shrub. It has been used since ancient times because of its medicinal as well as spiritual value.

Shrubs: Shrubs are the small woody plant with short, bushy stem.

For example : Hibiscus (china rose), Tulsi, Rose etc.

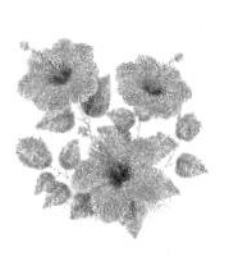  

Trees: Big and tall plants are called trees. Trees have strong and long branches.

For example : Mango, Neem, Banyan, etc.

Beside these, two other types of plants are climbers and creepers.

Climbers : Climbers are the plants which grow with the support of other tall objects.

For example : Grapevine, Money plant, etc.

Creepers: Creepers are the plants with weak stem. They grow along with ground, and also on the tree branches. For example: Pumpkin, Watermelon, etc.

Do you Know

- Herbs are used in foods, flavours, medicines and perfumes.

Amazing Facts

- The largest tree in the world is the **Red Wood Tree** . These trees can reach a height of 300 feet.

Red W[illegible]d Tree

Food items obtained from plants

Plants give fruits, vegetables & grains.

1. **Fruits** : Fruits are the part of plant that we eat.

   For example : Apple, Watermelon, Pineapple, Guava, etc.

2. **Vegetables** : Vegetables are the eatable parts of a plant. They can be eaten raw and also after cooking.

   For example : Potato, Onion, Brinjal, etc.

3. **Grains** : Grains can be eaten only after cooking.

   For example : Rice, Wheat, Pulses, etc.

Do You Know?

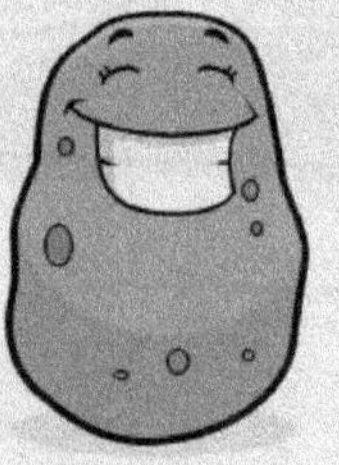

❖ Potatoes were the first food to be grow in space. In 1996, potato plants were taken into space with the space shuttle columbia.

Multiple Choice Questions

LEVEL- 1

1. **Which of the following trees have strong and woody branches?** **[Tricky]**
   (a) Mango (b) Money plant
   (c) Neem (d) both (a) and (c)
2. **Which of the following fruits contain only one seed?** **[Tricky]**
   (a) Apple (b) Mango
   (c) Papaya (d) Orange
3. **Which of the following is a feature of Shrubs?**
   (a) Short and busy stem (b) Long branches
   (c) Weak stem (d) All of the above
4. **Which of the following plant is a herb?**
   (a) Grapevine (b) Tulsi
   (c) Coriander (d) both (b) and (c)
5. **Which of the following type of plants have soft and weak stem and grows with the support of other tall objects?**
   (a) Herb (b) Climbers
   (c) Shrubs (d) None of these
6. **How many number of seeds are present in watermelon?**
   (a) One (b) Two
   (c) Four (d) Many
7. **Which of the following is a creeper?** **[Tricky]**
   (a)  Pumpkin (b)  Money Plant
   (c)  Grapevine (d) 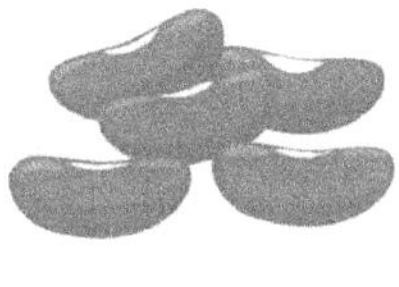 Bean

8. Which of the following statement is true?

(a) Apple contains one seed only
(b) Mango contains one seed only
(c) Potato is seedless
(d) both (b) and (c)

9. Which of the following is a vegetable?

(a) Pineapple
(b) Tomato
(c) Brinjal
(d) Both (a) and (b)

10. Which of the following is the most colourful part of a plant which changes into fruit?

(a) Root
(b) Leaves
(c) Flower
(d) Stem

11. Which of the following is an example of big and tall plant? [Tricky]

(a) Mango tree
(b) Banyan tree
(c) Rose plant
(d) both (a) and (b)

12. Which of the following can be eaten only after cooking?

(a) Fruits
(b) Grains
(c) Vegetables
(d) All of the above

13. Which of the following is the green part of a plant where food is made?

(a) Root
(b) Shoot **[Tricky]**
(c) Leaves
(d) Stem

14. Which of the following part of plant grows inside the surface of soil?

(a) Root
(b) Shoot **[Tricky]**
(c) Stem
(d) Leaves

15. Plants are held in the soil by ________.

(a) Flowers
(b) Stems
(c) Roots
(d) Leaves

16. Which of the following part of plant bears leaf and fruit?

(a) Roots
(b) Stem
(c) Flower
(d) All of these

17. Rice is an example of __________.

(a) Pulses
(b) Grain
(c) Brinjal
(d) None of these

18. Which of the following is not a part of plant?

(a) Root
(b) Leaves
(c) Shrubs
(d) All of these

19. I am a green fruit that tastes sour. My juice makes a very refreshing drink. Who am I? [Tricky]

(a)  Sweet lime

(b)  Pear

(c)  Kiwi

(d) All of these

20. Select the plant which is an odd one out in the group. [Tricky]

(a)  Barley

(b) Rice

(c)  Sugarcane

(d)  Wheat

21. Cabbage, lettuce and spinach are some of the _______ that we eat. [2013]

(a) Roots (b) Flowers
(c) Leaves (d) Pulses

22. Identify the plant in the given rhyme and select the correct option. [Critical Thinking]

I am erect and branchy, but I cannot grow tall.
I bear big red flowers, I am X as you call.

(a) X can be a climber like rose plant.
(b) X can be a shrub like hibiscus plant.
(c) X can be a creeper like '**malti**' plant.
(d) X can be a tree like **gulmohar** plant.

23. What is correct about the given plant? **[Tricky]**

(a) This plant is thin and tall.

(b) This plant grows along the ground.

(c) This plant needs support to stand up.

(d) This plant is strong and has thick trunk.

24. Select the incorrect match. **[2016]**

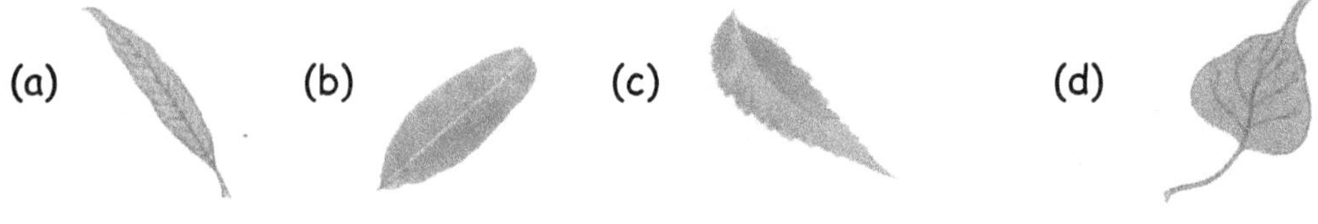

(a) Mango leaf (b) Banana leaf (c) Neem leaf (d) Pine leaf

25. Rashmi has pomegranate tree in the backyard of her home. One day, her elder brother plucked almost all flowers from the tree. This will result in ______________.

(a) Decreased growth of the tree.

(b) Reduced number of pomegranate fruits.

(c) Fall of leaves.

(d) None of these.

26. Which of the following is obtained from the same type of plant from which a pumpkin is obtained? **[2016]**

(a) (b) (c) (d)

27. What could be the reason for the poor growth of plant in pot F? **[2013, Tricky]**

(a) It was not given water regularly.

(b) It is filled with cement.

(c) It was placed in dark.

(d) All of these.

28.

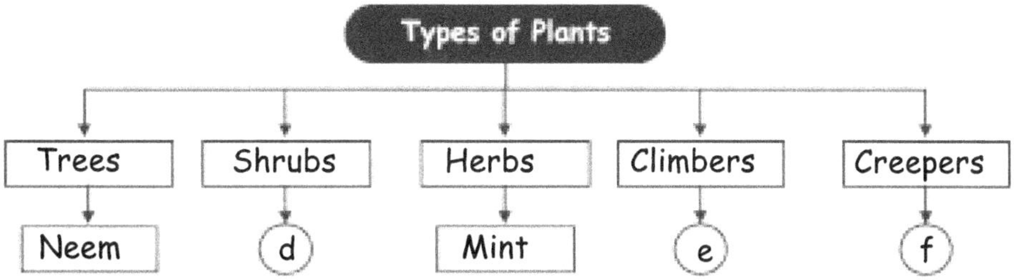

Types of Plants
- Trees → Neem
- Shrubs → d
- Herbs → Mint
- Climbers → e
- Creepers → f

Study the above given flowchart and select the correct option to fill empty spaces d, e and f. **[Critical Thinking]**

(a) d – Hibiscus, e – Pumpkin, f - Rose
(b) d – Rose, e – Pea, f - Spinach
(c) d – Rose, e – Grapevine, f - Pumpkin
(d) d – Grape, e – Hibiscus, f - Spinach

29. **Which of the following activities should you do?**
(a) Pluck flowers or leaves when you go to a park
(b) Write on the trunk of trees
(c) Grow more and more plants
(d) Throw stones at the fruits on trees

30. **Select the odd one out.** **[Tricky]**
(a) Orange (b) Carrot
(c) Turnip (d) Radish

31. **Cooking oil is obtained from ____________.** **[Tricky]**
(a)  (b) 
(c)  (d) All of these

32. **Ravi saw a plant in his garden which had beautiful flowers. When he tried to pluck a flower, his finger got pricked. The plat could be ________** **(2020)**
(a) Dahlia (b) Jasmine (c) Rose (d) Marigold

33. **Which of the following flowers is the part of a plant that bears floating leaf?**
(a)  (b)  (c)  (d)  **(2020)**

34. **Select the correct option to complete the given analogy.** **(2021)**

Peach : One-seeded fruit : : _______ : Few-seeded fruit

(a) Papaya (b) Pomegranate (c) Mango (d) Orange

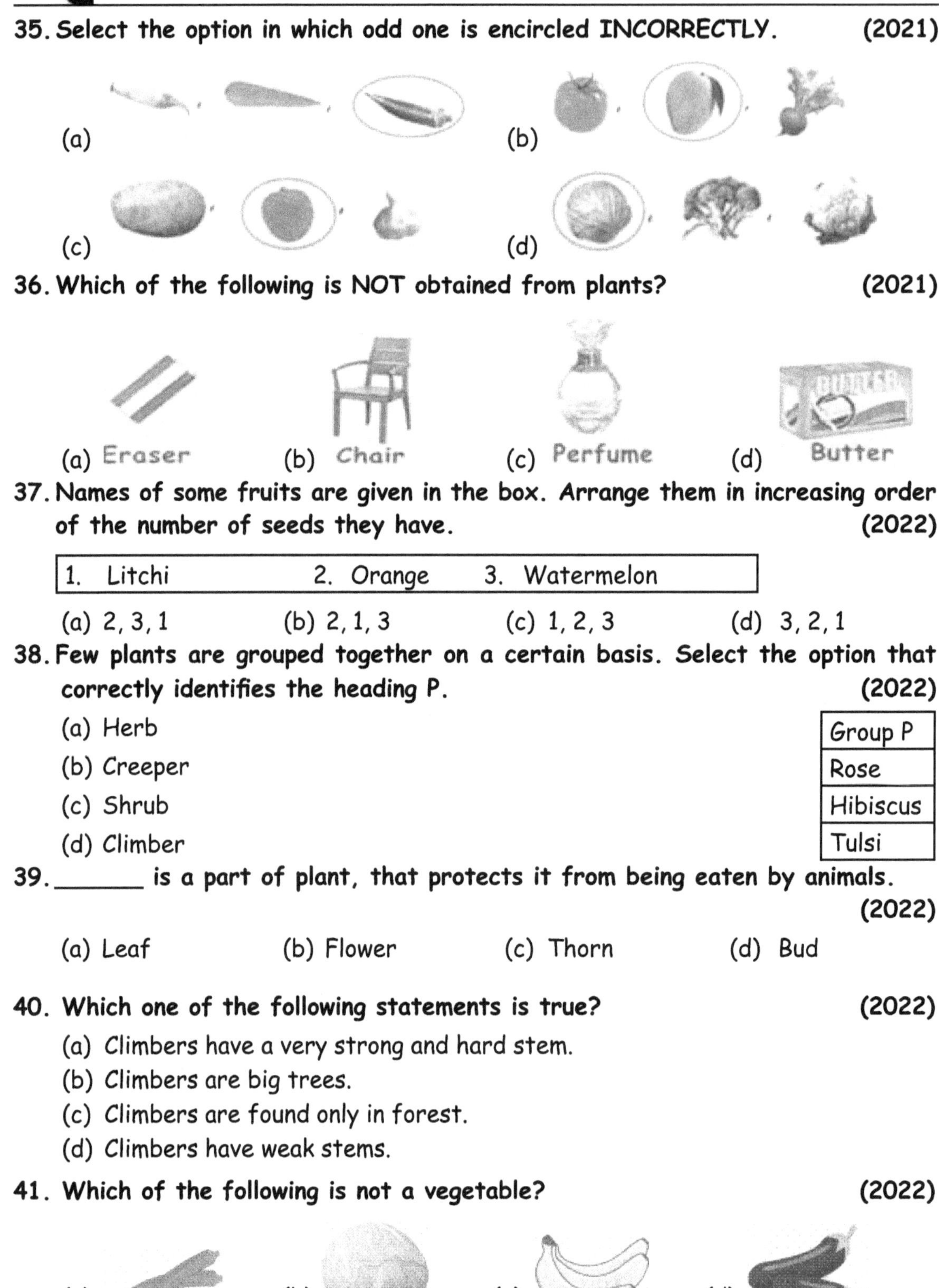

35. Select the option in which odd one is encircled INCORRECTLY. (2021)

(a) (b)

(c) (d)

36. Which of the following is NOT obtained from plants? (2021)

(a) Eraser (b) Chair (c) Perfume (d) Butter

37. Names of some fruits are given in the box. Arrange them in increasing order of the number of seeds they have. (2022)

1. Litchi	2. Orange	3. Watermelon

(a) 2, 3, 1 (b) 2, 1, 3 (c) 1, 2, 3 (d) 3, 2, 1

38. Few plants are grouped together on a certain basis. Select the option that correctly identifies the heading P. (2022)

Group P
Rose
Hibiscus
Tulsi

(a) Herb
(b) Creeper
(c) Shrub
(d) Climber

39. ______ is a part of plant, that protects it from being eaten by animals. (2022)

(a) Leaf (b) Flower (c) Thorn (d) Bud

40. Which one of the following statements is true? (2022)

(a) Climbers have a very strong and hard stem.
(b) Climbers are big trees.
(c) Climbers are found only in forest.
(d) Climbers have weak stems.

41. Which of the following is not a vegetable? (2022)

(a) (b) (c) (d)

42. **The food items shown below are:** **(2022)**

(a) vegetables (b) fruits (c) cereals (d) pulses

LEVEL- 2

1. **Read the sentence carefully and find True/False.** **[Critical Thinking]**
   A. Mango is an example of big tree.
   B. Flower is the most colourful part of plant.
   C. Flower changes into fruit.
   D. New plant develops from the leaves
   (a) TTFT (b) TFTF
   (c) TTTF (d) TTFF
2. **Which of the following parts of a mango plant grows into a new plant?**
   (a) Root (b) Shoot
   (c) Seed (d) Fruit
3. **Ram and Shyam were planting a plant in the garden, Rohan suddenly came and plucked it out. What would you do if you were in place of Rohan?**
   (a) Give water to plant. (b) Throw the plant in the Dustbin.
   (c) Throw stones on the plant. (d) None of these

Directions (Qs. 4 to 12): Fill in the blanks in the passage given below.

Big and tall plants are called _________ (4) _________. Shrubs are the small & woody plant which are _________ (5) _________ than trees. Stem provides _________ (6) _________ to the upper part of plant. _________ (7) _________ are the green part of plant where food is made. Flower is the most _________ (8) _________ part of a plant. Fruits are formed from _________ (9). Seed grows inside the _________ (10). Papaya has _________(11) _________ seeds. Brinjal and Potato are examples of _________ (12) _________

4. (a) herbs (b) shrubs
   (c) trees (d) roots
5. (a) smaller (b) taller
   (c) bigger (d) none of these
6. (a) roots (b) support
   (c) food (d) air

7. (a) Roots (b) Leaves
(c) Stem (d) Fruit

8. (a) tall (b) short
(c) beautiful (d) big

9. (a) flower (b) leaves
(c) roots (d) stem

10. (a) leaves (b) root
(c) fruit (d) vegetable

11. (a) one (b) two
(c) many (d) none of these

12. (a) fruits (b) vegetables
(c) grains (d) none of these

Directions (Qs. 13 to 17): Read the following paragraph and answer the following questions. [Critical Thinking]

Plants are our green friends which give us fruits, vegetables, flowers etc. Root, stem, and leaves, together form a plant. Roots are present under the soil and stem bears leaf, flower and fruits. Leaves prepare food for the plant. Fruits are that part of plant which we eat. Fruit contains seeds. Seeds are present inside the fruit. Some of the examples of fruits are : Apple, Mango, Banana, Pineapple, Papaya, etc.

13. What is the colour of plant?
(a) Green (b) Yellow
(c) Red (d) Pink

14. Seeds are present inside the ______.
(a) flower (b) leaves
(c) fruits (d) stem

15. Which of the following parts of plant cannot be seen?
(a) Roots (b) Stem
(c) Leaves (d) Fruits

16. ______ bears leaves and flower.
(a) Roots (b) Fruits
(c) Stem (d) None of these

17. I prepare food. Identify who I am?
(a) Root (b) Shoot (c) Leaves (d) Stem

18. Apple is a _______. It contains _______ inside them which give rise to a new _______. [Tricky]

(a) seed, fruit, flower (b) fruit, seeds, leaves
(c) fruit, leaves, fruit (d) fruit, seeds, plant

19. Match the following & mark the correct option.

	List I		List II
A.	Shrubs	1.	Mango, Apple
B.	Grain	2.	Rose, Hibiscus
C.	Fruit	3.	Money Plant, Beans
D.	Climbers	4.	Rice, Wheat

	A	B	C	D		A	B	C	D
(a)	2	4	3	1	(b)	2	4	1	3
(c)	4	1	2	3	(d)	3	2	4	1

20. Which of the following option replace 'X' and 'Y' in the table. **[Tricky]**

Fruit	Apple	Papaya
Herbs	Coriander	'X'
Grains	'Y'	Maize

(a) X - Potato, Y - Rice (b) X - Tulsi, Y - Papaya
(c) X - Grass, Y - Rice (d) X - Potato, Y - Tulsi

21. Based on the shape of the leaf 'X', which of these can be grouped together with it ? **[2013]**

Leaf 'X'

(a)  (b)  (c) 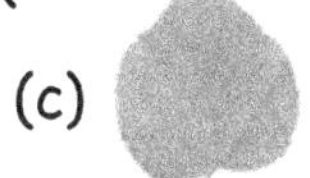 (d) 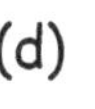

22. Which of the following part of the plant carries water & food from roots to other part of plant? **[Tricky]**
(a) Root (b) Stem (c) Flower (d) Leaves

23. Consider the following statements and choose the correct answer.

Statement A : Plants are living thing. They need food to grow.

Statement B : Creepers & climbers need support to grow.

Statement C : Maize and wheat are the examples of vegetables.

(a) Statement A is true and B, C is false. **[Critical Thinking]**
(b) Statement A, B and C are true.
(c) Statement A and B are true, C is false.
(d) Statement A, B, C are false.

24. Plants give us useful things such as fruits, vegetables, cereals, pulses, etc. The plant shown in the picture gives us _____. [2013]

(a) Cococa

(b) Tea

(c) Tee

(d) Cotton

25. From the box below, count and answer the total numbers of fruits and vegetables present in the box. [Tricky]

Apple	Brinjal	Mango	Maize
Rice	Pineapple	Wheat	Potato

(a) 4 (b) 5 (c) 6 (d) 3

26. Which of the following option is a true statement?

(a) Climbers have a very strong and hard stem.

(b) Climbers need support to grow.

(c) Climbers are found only in forest.

(d) None of the above.

27. Ramya planted plant X in her garden. She tied the stem of this plant to a pole placed besides it in the soil to help it grow. Which of the following could be plant X? [2016]

(a) (b) (c) (d)

28. Which of the following part of a plant gives rise to a new plant?

(a) Leaves (b) Root (c) Seed (d) Flower

29. Select the odd one out.

(a) Rice (b) Wheat (c) Maize (d) Tomato

30. Ruchi put a healthy herb in a well watered pot with good quality soil. Then she cut part X of this plant. She noticed that the plant withered in a day. Identify part X and select the correct option. [2016]

(a) Fruits (b) Roots (c) Leaves (d) Flowers

31. _______ are the lowest part of plant. Stem bears fruit, flower and ______.

(a) Roots, Fruit (b) Roots, Leaves **[Tricky]**

(c) Fruit, Stem (d) Leaves, Fruit

32. Which of the following is a herb?

(a) Rose Plant
(b) Mango Plant
(c) Grass
(d) Money Plant

33. Select the odd one out. **[2016]**

(a)  (b)  (c)  (d)

34. Which of the following is NOT a fruit?

(a)  (b)
(c)  (d)

35. The plant shown here provides us _____. **[2015]**

(a) Sugar
(b) Jaggery
(c) Oil
(d) Both a and b

36. We eat the seeds of __________. **[Tricky]**

(a)  (b) 
(c)  (d)

37. I became Cinderella's carriage. I am a P __ __ __ __ __ __

Fill up the blanks with the correct group of alphabets. **[Tricky]**

(a) M P I N K L
(b) O M E G R A
(c) O R R I D G
(d) U M P K I N

38. **Which of the following statements is incorrect about plants?** **[2015]**
   (a) Grapevine is a creeper plant.
   (b) Creepers are plants that grow along ground.
   (c) Money plant is a climber plant
   (d) Climbers are plants that climb up a support

39. **Select the correct option regarding the labelled parts of the plant as shown.** **[Critical Thinking]**

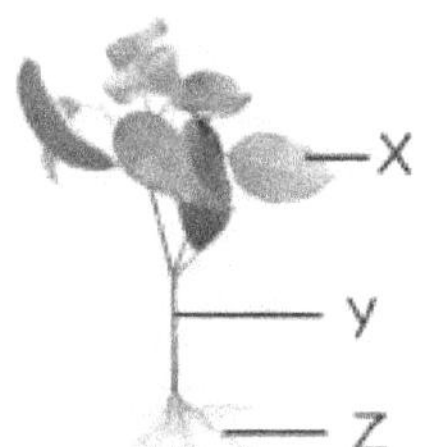

   (a) Mango is formed from Z.
   (b) Y makes food for the plant.
   (c) X anchors the plant into the ground.
   (d) We get ginger from Y and cabbage from X.

40. **Match the columns and select the correct option.** **[Tricky]**

Column I		Column II
(A) Shrubs	1.	Pumpkin plants
(B) Creepers	2.	Cucumber plant
(C) Climbers	3.	Tea plant

   (a) A-3, B-2, C-1 (b) A-1, B-2, C-3
   (c) A-1, B-3, C-2 (d) A-3, B-1, C-2

41. **Select the correct option regarding the parts X, Y and Z of plants as shown here.** **[2015]**

   (a) We get cabbage from Z.
   (b) We get carrot from X.
   (c) We get radish from X.
   (d) We get ginger from Y.

42. **Which of the following statements is INCORRECT?**
   (a) Wheat and rice are cereals. (b) Dals and grams are pulses.
   (c) Pea and onion are vegetables. (d) Mango has many seeds.

43. Here are some seeds given in the figure. Count and tell how many of each are there? [Tricky]

	Rajma	Pea	Corn	Gram
(a)	10	7	6	5
(b)	8	9	4	6
(c)	4	11	8	5
(d)	5	10	7	6

44. Raman is eating salad made of carrot, cucumber, broccoli and onion. He is actually eating __________ of plants. [2014]

(a) Roots and fruits

(b) Fruits, flowers and stem

(c) Fruits, stem, leaves and roots

(d) Roots, fruits, flowers and stem

45. **[Tricky]**

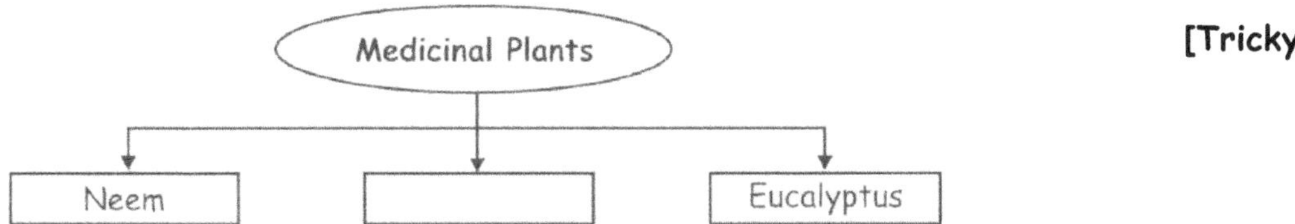

Study the above given flowchart. Which of the following options can correctly fill the empty box of the flowchart?

(a) Cotton
(b) Sugarcane
(c) Tulsi
(d) Maize

46. Which of the following is a common character of climbers and creepers? [Tricky]

(a) They have weak stems
(b) They grow along the ground
(c) They grow by coiling around a support
(d) They bear large flowers

47. Which part of the seed grows first when it sprouts? [2014]

(a) Roots (b) Stem (c) Leaf (d) Fruit

48. Based on the type of plant 'X', which amongst these plants can be grouped with it? [2014]

49. We eat different parts of different plants. Study the given classification chart and select the correct option to fill empty spaces d and e. (2020)

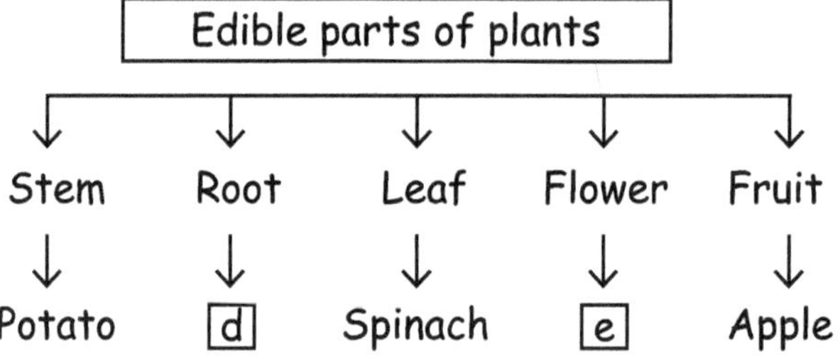

(a) d - Carrot, e - Broccoli

(b) d - Radish, e - Cabbage

(c) d - Carrot, e - Onion

(d) d - Ginger, e - Cauliflower

50. Four seeds (P, Q, R and S) of the same plant are shown in four different pots. Each of the pots is treated differently as shown in the table.

Which of these seeds wUl be ab'e to germinate? (2020)

(a) Seed Q only

(b) Seed R only

(c) Both seeds R and S

(d) Both seeds P and R

Seed	Air	Water	Sunlight
P	×	✓	×
Q	✓	✓	✓
R	✓	×	✓
S	✓	✓	×

51. **Unscramble the given letters to obtain the name of a vegetable.** **(2021)**

CIASNPH

Now, select the correct statement regarding it.

(a) Its edible part prepares food for the plant.

(b) Its edible part grows into a fruit.

(c) Its edible part absorbs minerals from the soil.

(d) Its edible part absorbs water from the soil.

52. **Which of the following statements is NOT correct about the given picture X?** **(2021)**

(a) It is a living thing but it cannot move from one place to another.

(b) It is a living thing and can breathe.

(c) It is a non-living thing that can prepare its own food.

(d) It is a living thing and can reproduce.

53. **Refer to the given flow chart and select the option that correctly identifies X, Y and Z.** **(2021)**

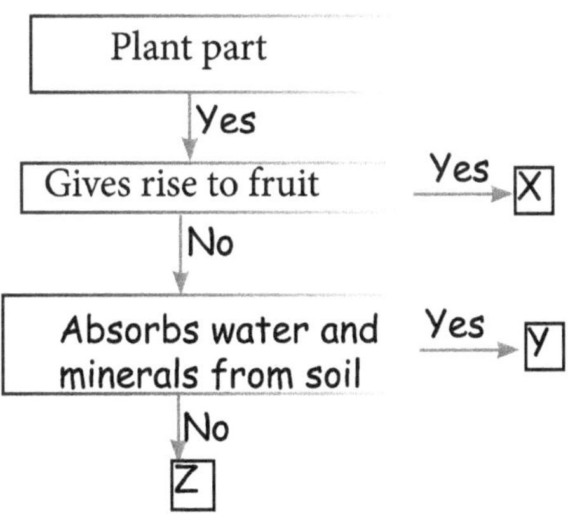

	X	Y	Z
(a)	Stem	Flower	Bud
(b)	Root	Leaf	Stem
(c)	Flower	Root	Leaf
(d)	Leaf	Stem	Root

54. Select the correct match. **(2022)**

(a) Kidney bean - Pulse
(b) Black pepper - Spice
(c) Ginger - Edible stem
(d) All of these.

55. Refer to the given diagram and select the option that correctly identifies seeds X and Y. **(2022)**

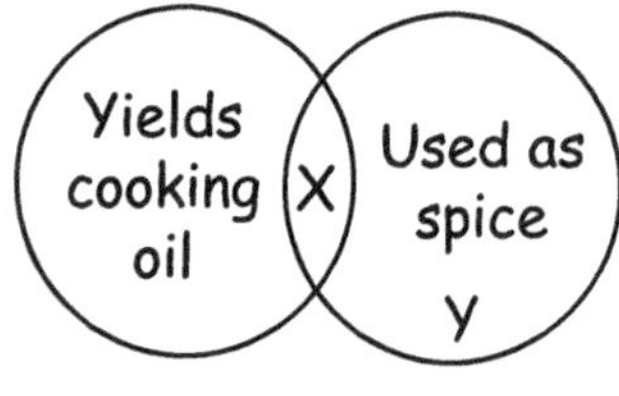

	X	Y
(a)	Coconut	Mustard
(b)	Mustard	Sunflower
(c)	Mustard	Coriander
(d)	Coriander	Sunflower

56. Which combination of statements is correct? **(2022)**

1. All plants and animals are living things.
2. Leaves are the important parts of plants.
3. Some plants grow in water.
4. Banana plant does not need water to grow.

(a) Only 1 and 2
(b) Only 1 and 3
(c) Only 2 and 4
(d) Only 1, 2 and 3

RESPONSE GRID

LEVEL 1

1. a b c d	2. a b c d	3. a b c d	4. a b c d	5. a b c d
6. a b c d	7. a b c d	8. a b c d	9. a b c d	10. a b c d
11. a b c d	12. a b c d	13. a b c d	14. a b c d	15. a b c d
16. a b c d	17. a b c d	18. a b c d	19. a b c d	20. a b c d
21. a b c d	22. a b c d	23. a b c d	24. a b c d	25. a b c d
26. a b c d	27. a b c d	28. a b c d	29. a b c d	30. a b c d
31. a b c d	32. a b c d	33. a b c d	34. a b c d	35. a b c d
36. a b c d	37. a b c d	38. a b c d	39. a b c d	40. a b c d
41. a b c d	42. a b c d			

LEVEL 2

1. a b c d	2. a b c d	3. a b c d	4. a b c d	5. a b c d
6. a b c d	7. a b c d	8. a b c d	9. a b c d	10. a b c d

11. a b c d	12. a b c d	13. a b c d	14. a b c d	15. a b c d
16. a b c d	17. a b c d	18. a b c d	19. a b c d	20. a b c d
21. a b c d	22. a b c d	23. a b c d	24. a b c d	25. a b c d
26. a b c d	27. a b c d	28. a b c d	29. a b c d	30. a b c d
31. a b c d	32. a b c d	33. a b c d	34. a b c d	35. a b c d
36. a b c d	37. a b c d	38. a b c d	39. a b c d	40. a b c d
41. a b c d	42. a b c d	43. a b c d	44. a b c d	45. a b c d
46. a b c d	47. a b c d	48. a b c d	49. a b c d	50. a b c d
51. a b c d	52. a b c d	53. a b c d	54. a b c d	55. a b c d
56. a b c d				

Solutions with Explanation

LEVEL 1

1. (d) Mango and Neem tree are tall and big plants. They have strong and woody branches, whereas money plant has soft stem.
2. (b) Mango fruit contains one seed only.
3. (a) Shrubs contain short & bushy stem.
4. (d) Coriander and Tulsi are herbs, Grapevine is a climber.
5. (b) Climbers have soft & weak stem which needs the support of another plant to grow.
6. (d) Water-Melon contains many seeds.
7. (a) Pumpkin is a creeper
8. (d) Apple contains many seeds, Mango contains one seed & Potato is a vegetable, does not contain seed.
9. (c) Brinjal is a vegetable while pineapple, and tomato are fruits.
10. (c) Flowers are the most colourful part of a plant that change into fruit.
11. (d) Mango & banyan are big and tall plants. Rose is a shrub.
12. (b) Grains can be eaten only after cooking.
13. (c) Leaves are the green part of plant where food is prepared.
14. (a) Root grows inside the surface of soil.
15. (b)

16. (b) Stem bears leaves, flowers and fruits.

17. (b) Rice is an example of grain.

18. (c) Shrubs is not a part of plant.

19. (a)

20. (c)

21. (c) We eat leaves of cabbage, lettuce and spinach.

22. (b)

23. (c)

24. (d) Option (d) is peepal Leaf.

25. (b)

26. (d) Both pumpkin and water- melon (Option d) are creepers. Pea (Option b) and grapevine (Option c) are climbers whereas maize (Option a) is a large herb grain plant.

27. (d) 28. (c) 29. (c) 30. (a) 31. (d)

32. (c) 33. (b)

34. (d) Orange is a few seeded fruit.

35. (b) Mango is a fruit while other two are vegitables.

36. (d) Butter is obtained from animals.

37. (c)

38. (c) These all are shrubs.

39. (c)

40. (d)

41. (c) 42. (b)

LEVEL 2

1. (c) Statements (A, B, C) are true and statement D is false as new plant develops from the seeds.

2. (c) Seeds of a mango tree grows into a new plant.

3. (a) We should not pluck the plants.
4. (c) Trees
5. (a) Smaller
6. (b) Support
7. (b) Leaves
8. (c) beautiful
9. (a) flower
10. (c) fruit
11. (c) many
12. (b) vegetables
13. (a) The colour of plant is green.
14. (c) Seeds are present inside the fruits.
15. (d) Roots are present under the soil and so cannot be seen.
16. (c) Stem bears flowers and leaves.
17. (c) Leaves prepare food.
18. (d) Apple is a fruit. It contains seeds inside them which grows into a new plant.
19. (b)
20. (c) Tulsi is an example of herb & rice is an example of Grain.
21. (b) Leaf X and leaf in option B both have five lobed shape.
22. (b) Stem carries water & foods from root to other part of plant.
23. (c) Statement A & B are true and Statement C is false as Maize & Wheat are the examples of grains.
24. (d) The plant shown in the picture is a cotton plant. It gives us cotton fibres.
25. (b) Total number of fruits & vegetables are 5.

    No. of fruit = 3 (apple, mango, pineapple)

    No. of vegetable = 2 (brinjal, potato)
26. (b) Climbers are the plants with soft and weak stem. Climbers grow with the support of another plant.

27. **(b)** Money plant is a climber which can climb up a support and reach heights. If a pole is placed beside money plant then instead of spreading to the ground it will coil around the pole to spread to heights.

28. **(c)** Seeds give rise to a new plant.

29. **(d)** Rice, wheat and maize all are the examples of grain and tomato is a fruit.

30. **(b)** If roots of a herb are cut then it will not be able to absorb water from the soil. Without water the plant will die in some time.

31. **(b)** Roots are the lowest part of plant. Stem bears fruits, flower & leaves.

32. **(c)** Grass is an example of herb.

33. **(d)** Radish (Option a), carrot (Option b) and beetroot (Option c) are modified underground roots that store food. Onion (Option d) is a modified stem with leaves which store food. Hence onion (d) is the odd one in the group.

34. **(d)**

35. **(d)** The plant shown here of sugarcane. Sugar and Jaggery are made from sugarcane stem juice.

36. **(b)** 37. **(d)**

38. **(a)** Grapevine is a climber plant which takes support of other plants, sticks or walls to climb up. Option b, c and d are all correct about plants.

39. **(d)** 40. **(a)**

41. **(d)** Here 'X' is leaf, 'Y' is stem and 'Z' is root. We get radish and carrot from roots (Z), ginger from stem (Y) and cabbage from leaves (X).

42. **(d)** 43. **(d)** 44. **(d)** 45. **(c)**

46. **(a)** 47. **(a)** 48. **(c)**

49. **(a)** 50. **(a)**

51. **(a)** Spinach

52. **(c)** Cactus is a living thing, that can prepare its own food.

53. **(c)** Flower give rise to fruits. Roots absorb water and minerals from soil. Leaves does not absorbs water and minerals from soil.

54. **(d)** Ginger is an stem. All of these are correctly match.

55. **(c)** Mustard is used as cooking oil. Coriander is used as spice.

56. **(d)**

3 CHAPTER FOREWORD

Did you see that big lion in the zoo?

Did you see how the monkey jumped from one tree to the other? You must have seen different animals in the zoo, in your house and everywhere.

Identify the name of the animal. Then circle the first letter of the name. Spell the alphabets in proper order.

1. U C K D ______

2.  O I N L ______

3.  P H A N T E L E ______

4. K A S N E ______

5.  Y E M O N K ______

When you finish reading this chapter, you will be able to identify different types of animals, birds and insects. You will also know many interesting facts about the world of animals.

3 Chapter

Animals

LEARNING OBJECTIVES

This lesson will help you to:

- Gain knowledge about animals.
- Learn about different types of animals and their habitats.
- Study about birds and their features.
- Know about insects.

INTRODUCTION

You must have seen cows eating grass, dogs and cats roaming around, houseflies and mosquitoes flying in your house.

Some of these animals are large in size and some are small. These animals help us in many ways. Let us study about these animals in details.

Animals : There are different types of animals around us. Some animals live on ground, for example: Cow, Horse. Some animals live in water, for example: fishes. Some animals live on trees, for example : Monkey. Some are kept at our home, for example : Cat, Dog, Rabbit.

TYPES OF ANIMALS

On the basis of their home, animals are divided into following types:

1. Wild Animals
2. Domestic Animals
3. Aquatic Animals

(1) **Wild Animals:** The animals that live in forest are called wild animals. For example : Lion, Tiger, Fox, Giraffe, Cheetah.

(2) **Domestic Animals :** Domestic animals are kept at our home and also in farms. They are also known as **pets**. For example: Dog, Cat, Rabbit.

Some domestic animals are very useful to us in many ways. For example : Cow, Buffalo and Goat give us milk, Hen gives egg.

Some domestic animals are used in transportation. For example: Horse, Donkey, Ox, Camel.

Camel can live in desert because it has a hump which can store water for many days.

(3) **Aquatic Animals:** Animals that live in water are called aquatic animals. For Example : Fish, Dolphin, Frog, Crocodile, Tortoise.

Real Life Examples

- Dog is considered as the most faithful animal in the world.
- Cats are one of the most popular pets in the world. There are over 500 million domestic cats in the world.

Misconcept/Concept

- **Misconcept** - All the birds can fly.

  Concept - All the birds cannot fly. Many birds, for example : Ostrich and Penguin cannot fly. They are flightless birds.

Amazing Facts

- The tongue of giraffe is too long that it can clean its ear with its tongue.

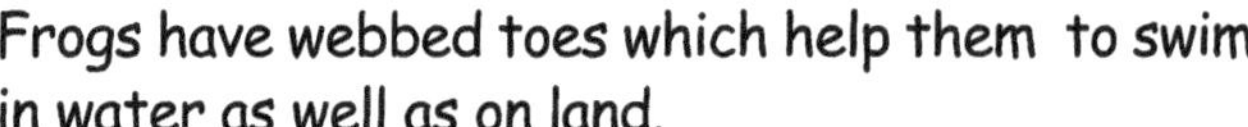

Frogs have webbed toes which help them to swim in water as well as on land.

BIRDS

You might have seen some creatures flying in the sky. These are the birds.

- Birds are the living creatures that can fly in the air, and have feathers, wings & beak. Birds have no teeth.
- Birds have wings which help them to fly in air.
- Birds lay eggs.

For example : Parrot, Eagle, Ostrich, Peacock, Crow, Pigeon.

Birds like Duck & Swan can swim in water.

INSECTS

Have you seen some very small creatures crawling on the ground and flying in the air. These are known as insects. Insects are the small creatures that have six legs and 0 to 2 pairs of wings.

For example : Housefly, Mosquito, Butterfly, Ant, Honey bee.

Amazing Facts

- Butterflies do not have mouth instead they have a long straw, like organ , called probosis by which they tack their food.

Historical Preview

- Do you know, we all (commonly known as human beings) have been evolved from animals.

HOME OF ANIMALS, INSECTS and BIRDS

Animals need home to live in. For example: rabbit lives in burrow, lion lives in den.

Let us know more about their homes:

	ANIMAL	HOME
1.	Lion	Den
2.	Tiger	Den/Lair
3.	Bear	Den
4.	Fox	Den
5.	Dog	Kennel
6.	Cat	Cattery

Do you Know?

- Tiger is known as the national animal of India & Peacock is the national bird of India.
- Cheetah is the fastest running land animal.
- Elephant is the largest land animal.
- Some animals can live both on land and water.

For eg. Tortoise, Frog.

Do you Know?

- Fishes have fins that help them to swim in water.

7.	 Rabbit	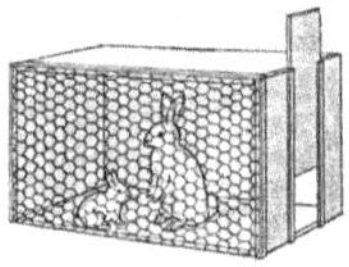 Hutch
8.	 Horse	 Stable
9.	 Hen	 Coope, Run
10.	 Honey Bee	 Hive
11.	 Pigs	 Sty

Multiple Choice Questions

LEVEL 1

1. **Which of the following is an example of wild animal?**

   (a) Cow (b) Tiger (c) Hen (d) Goat

2. **Which of the following bird runs very fast but cannot fly?** **[Tricky]**

   (a) Crow (b) Parrot (c) Ostrich (d) Peacock

3. **Which of the following animal lives in water?**

   (a) Parrot (b) Crocodile

   (c) Frog (d) Both (b) and (c)

4. **Which of the following animals live at our home?**

   (a) Dog (b) Lion (c) Kangaroo (d) Giraffe

5. **We get wool from _______.**

   (a) Horse (b) Sheep (c) Cow (d) Buffalo

6. **Which of the following animal is used for transportation purpose?**

   (a) Horse (b) Donkey (c) Ox (d) All of these

7. **Which of the following animal lays eggs?**

   (a) Crow (b) Goat (c) Rabbit (d) Cat

8. **Which of the following animals lives on tree?**

   (a) Lion (b) Dog

   (c) Monkey (d) None of these

9. **Which one of the following is wrong match of animals and their homes?** **[Tricky]**

   (a) Cat - Kennel (b) Horse - Stable

   (c) Rabbit - Hutch (d) Tiger - Lair

10. **Giraffe is a/an _________ animal.**

    (a) Wild (b) Aquatic (c) Domestic (d) Pet

11. Which of the following animal lives here? **[Tricky]**

(a) Butterfly (b) Crocodile (c) Parrot (d) Ostrich

12. Which of the following is TRUE about birds? **[Tricky]**

(a) Birds have wings (b) Birds have beak

(c) Birds lay eggs (d) All of these

13.

These animals are ____________. **[Tricky]**

(a) farm animals (b) wild animals

(c) water animals (d) domestic animals

14. I have wings, I can fly, I don't have teeth. Guess who I am? **[Tricky]**

(a) Ostrich (b) Parrot (c) Ant (d) Fish

15. Which of the following is the national animal of India?

(a) Lion (b) Tiger (c) Zebra (d) Giraffe

16. Which of the following is a bird?

(a) Dolphin (b) Peacock (c) Butterfly (d) All of these

17. **Which of the following statement is TRUE?** **[Tricky]**

(a) Horse is a wild animal (b) Horse is a domestic animal

(c) Cow is an aquatic animal (d) Giraffe is used in transportation

18. **Name X and Y?** **[Tricky]**

Y : Animal with six legs.

X : Animal with six legs as well as wings.

(a) X – Louse, Y – Cockroach (b) X – Flea, Y - Mosquito

(c) X – Cockroach, Y – Flea (d) X – Termite, Y - Grasshopper

19. **Which of these birds can run very fast, but it cannot fly?** **[Tricky]**

(a) (b) (c) (d)

20. **Starting from first letter, cross out every alternate letter and identify the name of the animal that can live in both land and water.** **[Tricky]**

(a) EMAOLNSKUEVY (b) TOTCITFOCPLUMS

(c) TFGRSOUG (d) HFSITSLH

21. **Which of these animals eats both plants and other animals?**

(a) Bear (b) Squirrel (c) Lizard (d) Giraffe

22. I will look like a frog when I will grow up. **Who am I?** **[Tricky]**

(a) Calf (b) Lamb (c) Joey (d) Tadpole

23. **Study the given pattern carfully.** **[Tricky]**

KNIVE : BEES : HIVE

Which of these follow(s) the given pattern?

(1) WEST : BIRD : NEST

(2) FURROW : RABBIT : BURROW

(3) PEN : ELEPHANT : DEN

(a) 1 only (b) 1 and 2 (c) 3 only (d) 2 and 3

24. We make homes for domestic animals. The home shown in the given figure is called ________. [2015, Tricky]

(a) Stable (b) Shed (c) Coop (d) Kennel

25. Study the given flow chart and answer the questions that follow: [2013]

(a) Where can you place animal 'X' who has eight legs ?

(b) Where can you place animal 'Y' who give us honey ?

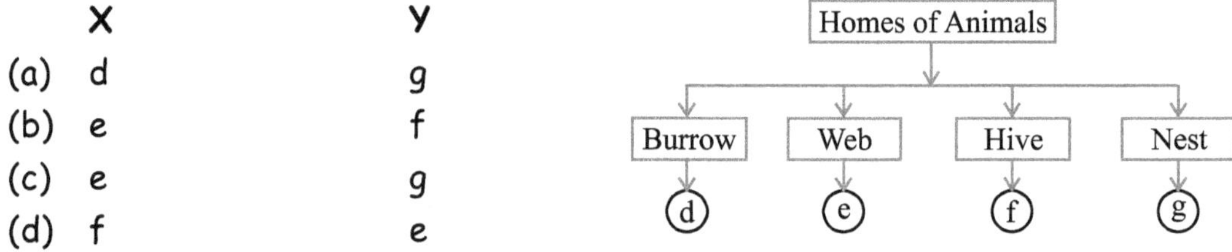

	X	Y
(a)	d	g
(b)	e	f
(c)	e	g
(d)	f	e

26. Some birds can swim, for example ___________.

(a) Swan (b) Duck

(c) Sparrow (d) Both (a) and (b)

27. Which of these is a correct match ? [2013]

	Domestic animal	Wild animal
(a)	Zebra	Elephant
(b)	Sheep	Crocodile
(c)	Kangaroo	Octopus
(d)	Horse	Hen

28. As I slither
through the grass, I say "HISS",
to those who pass!
I can be poisonous if I bite!
I am a fearful sight!

Who am I? [Tricky]

(a)  (b)  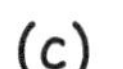 (c)   (d) 

29. Domestic animals can be kept in our homes as well as in ________ .

(a) forest (b) water (c) village (d) farms

30. Select the INCORRECT pair of animal and its home. [2015]

(a) Squirrel - Tree holes (b) Owl - Nest

(c) Lion - Den (d) Horse - Stable

31. I have yellow and brown stripes on my body. I am the National Animal of India. Who am I?

(a) Lion (b) Cheetah (c) Tiger (d) Zebra

32. Which picture shows correct behavior towards animals?

(a)  (b)

(c)  (d) None of these

33. Select the INCORRECT match out of the following. [2015]

(a) Lion - Mane (b) Elephant - Trunk

(c) Wolf - Muzzle (d) Penguin - Whiskers

34. Select the bird that is an odd one among the following. [2016]

(a)  (b)  (c)  (d)

35. Ali made four groups of domestic animals, but he placed one wild animal in one of the groups. Identify this group and select the correct options. [2016]

(a) Cow, Buffalo, Goat (b) Horse, Sheep, Hen

(c) Hen, Goat, Buffalo (d) Frog, Cow, Horse

36. Select the option that correctly fills the blanks in the given paragraph. [2016]

Birds have __________ legs, while insects have __________ legs. Spider has ________ legs thus it __________ an insect.

(a) 2, 6, 6, is (b) 2, 8, 8, is

(c) 2, 6, 8, is not (d) 2, 8, 6, is not

37. **Study the given relationship. Which amongst these can be 'X'?** [2014]

Owl : Owlet : : Goat : X

(a) Joey (b) Calf
(c) Lamb (d) Kid

38. **Identify the sounds of the given animals X and Y.** (2018)

	X	Y
(a)	Growl	Trumpet
(b)	Moo	Neigh
(c)	Bray	Chatter
(d)	Quack	Bark

39. **Which of these animals has NO legs?** (2018)

(a) Ant (b) Butterfly (c) Earthworm (d) Lizard

40. **Study the given relationship**

Select the option which correctly identifies X. Kennel : Dog :: Coop :X (2018)

(a) Cow (b) Pig (c) Cat (d) Hen

41. **Select and INCORRECT pair.** (2018)

	Animal	Group
(a)	Lion	Pride
(b)	Ant	Army
(c)	Elephant	Flock
(d)	Dog	Pack

42. **Which of the following animals gives birth to young ones?** (2019)

(a)  (b)  (c)  (d)

43. **Select the animal whose sound is called 'trumpet'.** (2019)

(a)  (b)  (c)  (d)

44. **Which of the following is both plant and animal eater?** (2020)

(a)  (b)  (c)  (d)

45. **Select the correct match.** (2020)

	Animal	Young one
A.	Elephant	Cub
B.	Lion	Calf
C.	Dog	Chick
D.	Horse	Foal

46. I live in shed. Who am I? (2020)

(a) (b) (c) (d)

47. All the given animals build a home to live in except (2020)

(a) Spider (b) Bee (c) Monkey (d) Bird

48. Select the suitable heading for group X arid group Y. (2020)

Group X
Cow, Horse, Sheep

Group Y
Dog, Cat, Rabbit

	X	Y
A.	Pet animals	Farm animals
B.	Domestic aniirrals	Farm animals
C.	Domestic triirrals	Wild animals
D.	Farm anmals	Pet animals

49. Binny did a study on two animals X and Y. At the end of her study, she made the observations as shown in the given table. (2020)

Observations	Animal X	Animal Y
Animal makes its own home	×	✓
Animals lays eggs	×	✓
Animal eats only other animals	✓	×

Select the option that correctly identifies animals x and Y?

	Animal X	Animal Y
A.	Bear	Snake
B.	Butterfly	Frog
C.	Lion	crow
D.	Horse	Mosquito

50. Which of the following is the young one of the animal shown in the given picture? (2021)

(a) Infant

(b) Calf

(c) Joey

(d) Foal

51. Select the option that can be placed in the same group as animal X. (2021)

(a) (b) 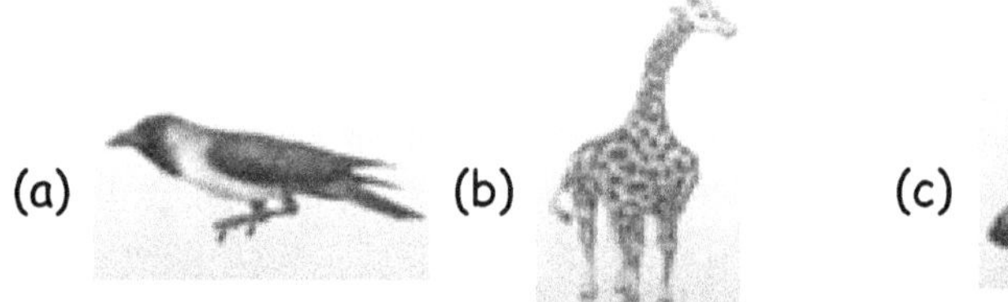
(c) (d) 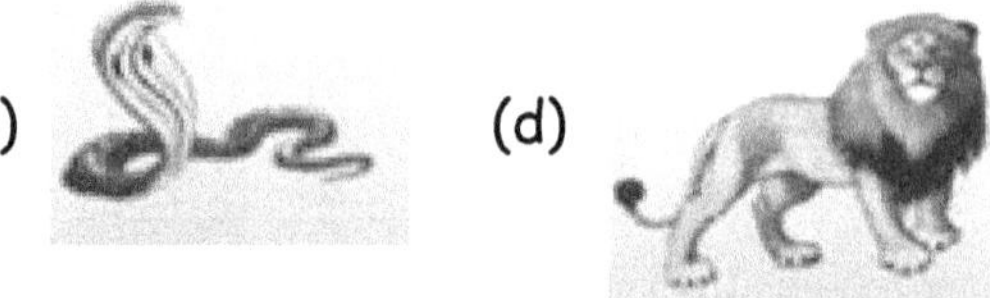

52. Which of the following is an INCORRECT match? **(2021)**

(a) Bear - Sloth
(b) Goat - Tribe
(c) Frog - Swarm
(d) Giraffe- Tower

53. Which of the following animals gives birth to young ones? **(2021)**

(a) 
(b) 
(c) 
(d) 

54. I can live both on land and in water. My group is called army. Who am I? **(2022)**

(a) 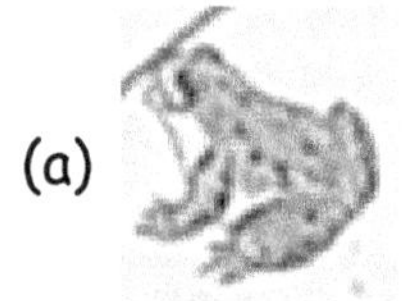
(b) 
(c) 
(d) 

55. The baby of the animal X shown in the given picture is called the same as the baby of a ______. **(2022)**

(a) 
(b) 
(c) 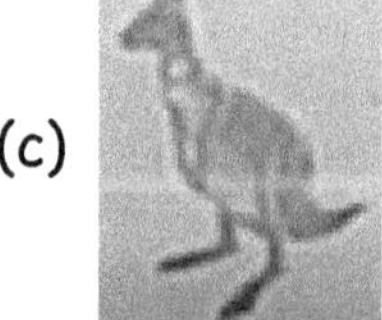
(d) 

56. What is the name of the water animal shown below? **(2022)**

(a) Shark
(b) Octopus
(c) Crocodile
(d) Hippopotamus

57. Which of the following animals has wings? **(2022)**

(a) 1

(b) 2

(c) Both 1 and 2 have wings.

(d) Neither 1 nor 2 has wings.

(1) (2)

58. Find the missing term in the given series. **(2022)**

7 9 13 19 ? 37

(a) 25 (b) 27 (c) 30 (d) 32

LEVEL- 2

1. Which of the following is a fast running animal?

(a) Camel (b) Cheetah (c) Ox (d) All of these

2. Which of the following animals gives us milk?

(a) Cow (b) Giraffe (c) Horse (d) Ox

3. Which of the following is the largest land animal? **[Tricky]**

(a) Dolphin (b) Elephant (c) Giraffe (d) Camel

4. Which of the following is the small animal?

(a) Lion (b) Cheetah (c) Dog (d) Elephant

5. **'X' is the biggest animal on land but 'Y' is the biggest animal on Earth.**

[2013]

Among the given animals 'd, e, f and g'. Identify 'X' and 'Y'.

	X	Y
(a)	f	d
(b)	g	f
(c)	e	d
(d)	d	f

d e f g

6. **Fish live in water. They swim with the help of their fins. Some animals live on land. There are some animals like frog, hippopotamus and crocodile which are found both on land and in water. Most birds can fly with the help of their wings. Animals with six legs are called insects. [2013]**

   The above passage best describes that the animals ___________.

   (a) Are of different sizes (b) Are of different kinds
   (c) Are found in different locations (d) Both b and c

7. **Study the given relationship. Which of the following can be placed in the blank ? [2015]**

   Stable : horse : : Sty : _____

   (a) Pig (b) Cow (c) Hen (d) Sheep

8. **Which of the following eats flesh of dead animals? [Tricky]**

   (a) Pigeon (b) Vulture (c) Horse (d) Parrot

9. **Identify the given picture:**

   (a) Fish
   (b) Butterfly
   (c) Ant
   (d) Mosquito

10. **Read the following statements and choose the correct answer. [Tricky]**

    1. **Cow is a Domestic Animal.**
    2. **Cow gives us Milk.**
    3. **Cow lives in water.**
    4. **Rabbit helps in transportation.**

    (a) Statements 1, 4 are false statements 2, 3 are true.
    (b) Statements 1, 2, 3 are true, statement 4 is false.
    (c) Statements 1, 2 are true and 3, 4 are false.
    (d) All the statements are true.

11. **Insects have ________ legs, four ________ and ________ teeth. [Tricky]**

    (a) six, wings, zero (b) four, beak, two
    (c) three, three, zero (d) six, beaks, three

Directions (Qs. 12 to 21): Read the passage given below and fill in the blanks by choosing the correct option. [Critical Thinking]

The animals which live in _______ (12)_____ are called wild animals. ________ (13)_______ and _______(14) _______ are the examples of wild animals. Wild animals eat the _______ (15) _______ of other animals. Animals kept at our home are known as _______(16) _______ animals. _______(17) _______ can live both on land and in water. _______(18) _______ is used in transportation. Birds are the living creatures. They have _______(19) _______. Birds have no _______(20) _______. Rabbit is a _______ (21) _______ animal.

12.	(a)	sea	(b)	forest	(c)	lake	(d)	trees
13.	(a)	Rabbit	(b)	Dog	(c)	Lion	(d)	Hen
14.	(a)	tiger	(b)	horse	(c)	cow	(d)	none of these
15.	(a)	fruit	(b)	flesh	(c)	flower	(d)	leaves
16.	(a)	domestic	(b)	wild	(c)	water	(d)	none of these
17.	(a)	Cheetah	(b)	Tortoise	(c)	Monkey	(d)	Both (a) and (b)
18.	(a)	Giraffe	(b)	Dog	(c)	Tiger	(d)	Camel
19.	(a)	tongue	(b)	feather	(c)	teeth	(d)	all of these
20.	(a)	teeth	(b)	eyes	(c)	beak	(d)	wings
21.	(a)	pet	(b)	wild	(c)	water	(d)	none of these

22. Match the column (I) with column (II).

Column I		Column II	
A.	Lion	1.	Stable
B.	Dog	2.	Den
C.	Horse	3.	Nest
D.	Bird	4.	Kennel

	A	B	C	D
(a)	1	2	3	4
(b)	2	3	4	1
(c)	2	4	1	3
(d)	1	4	3	2

23. Identify 'Y': **[Tricky]**

Y is an animal which lives in water and land.

(a) Monkey (b) Dolphin (c) Frog (d) Lion

24. Choose the correct answer. **[Tricky]**

(a) Animals have feathers (b) Birds have feathers

(c) Birds have teeth (d) Insects have feathers

25. How many names of animals, birds and insects are hidden in the given word grid? **[Tricky]**

D	E	H	L	I	D	U	C	K
E	L	E	P	H	A	N	T	A
E	S	N	A	K	E	M	U	W
R	A	C	U	R	K	E	Y	I

(a) 6 (b) 8 (c) 9 (d) 10

26. **Study the given word grid to find the number of animals:** **[2015]**

(a) That eat animals only.

(b) That eat plants only.

	a	b
(a)	4	3
(b)	3	2
(c)	2	3
(d)	2	4

P	N	C	Z	M	L
L	I	O	N	V	T
S	G	W	U	B	C
N	O	B	E	A	R
A	A	M	J	Q	O
K	T	I	G	E	W
E	W	O	L	F	X

27. **Unscramble the given words and select the option that gives name of the home of animal shown here.** **[2016]**

(a) ENTS

(b) ESALTB

(c) SDEH

(d) POOC

28. **Which animals are most likely to live here?** **[2014]**

(a) Parrot, Frog, Rabbit, Ant

(b) Parrot, Rabbit, Sparrow, Fish

(c) Hippopotamus, Crocodile, Grasshopper, Snake

(d) Crow, Squirrel, Snake, Ant

29. **The given animals can be grouped together because they all __________.** **[2014]**

(a) Live in water

(b) Have feathers

(c) Have webbed feet

(d) Live in cold place

30. **Ravi went to a circus with his friends. He saw some people throwing stones at the animals. In such a situation, what should Ravi do?**

(a) He should watch people throwing stone at animals.

(b) He should also start throwing stones.

(c) Stop those people who are throwing stones at animals.

(d) None of these

31. Which of the following options replaces 'X' and 'Y' in the following. [Tricky]

Wild Animal	Bear	Tiger
Pets	'X'	Cat
Birds	Peacock	'Y'

(a) X = Rabbit, Y = butterfly
(b) X = Eagle, Y = Parrot
(c) X = Deer, Y = Eagle
(d) X = Dog, Y = Eagle

Direction (Qs. 32 to 35): See the diagram carefully and answer the following question. [Critical Thinking]

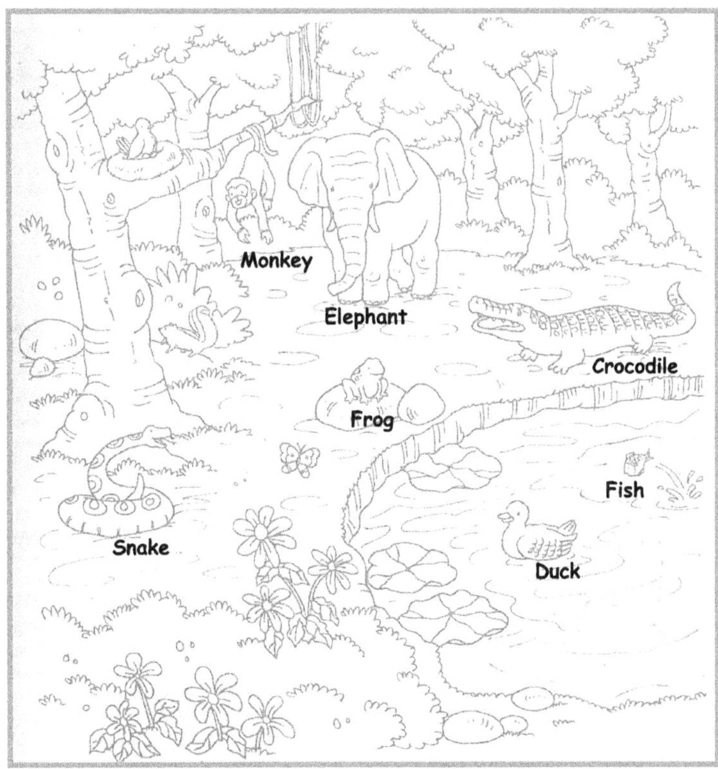

32. Which of the animals shown in the picture live in water?

(a) Duck (b) Fish (c) Frog (d) All of these

33. Which animal in the picture lives on tree?

(a) Tiger (b) Snake (c) Monkey (d) Crocodile

34. Which of the animals in the picture can live both in water and on land?

(a) Elephant (b) Frog (c) Butterfly (d) Monkey

35. Which animal in the picture is a wild animal?

(a) Crocodile (b) Duck (c) Elephant (d) Tortoise

36. From the given box, count & answer the total number of Domestic animals, birds & aquatic animals present in the box. **[Tricky]**

Cow	Hen	Lion	Cheetah	Parrot
Ostrich	Rabbit	Butterfly	Monkey	Frog

(a) 3 (b) 4 (c) 6 (d) 2

37. Which of the following is a correct match?

	Animal	**Type of food they eat**
(a)	Eagle	Plants
(b)	Deer	Both plants and flesh of other animals
(c)	Mouse	Flesh of other animals
(d)	Hen	Grains

38. "It lived by the waterside, **[Tricky]**
And little did it lack,
But when we asked, "How do you do?"
It only said, "Quack-Quack".
Which animal is being referred to in the above rhyme?

(a) Frog (b) Duck (c) Crocodile (d) Turtle

39. Which of these animals has no legs?

(a) Butterfly (b) Earthworm (c) Snake (d) Both (b) and (c)

40. Which of the following statements is correct?

(a) Birds have two wings and two legs (b) Mouse has two legs
(c) Insects have eight legs (d) Bear has two legs

41. Unscramble the given letters to get the names of the homes of the given animals X and Y. **[Critical Thinking]**

	X	Y
(a)	TENS	BLATES
(b)	NETS	LABEST
(c)	ENST	TABLES
(d)	NEST	STABLE

42. Which one of the following comes under the category of both farm and domestic animals? **[Tricky]**

(a) Tiger (b) Ox (c) Fox (d) Hyena

43. Choose the correct one out of the following statements?

(a) Insects have two legs (b) Birds lay eggs
(c) wild animals do not eat flesh (d) frog can only live in water

44. Fold is the home of_____. **[Tricky]**

(a) Lion (b) Snake (c) Tiger (d) Sheep

45. Just see the pictures and identify which one has fin?

(a)  (b)  (c) (d)

46. Unscramble the given letter groups to get the name of home of an animal the has six legs, can fly and gives us honey. **(2018)**

(a) NEENKL (b) UROBRW (c) TBESAL (d) HEVIEBE

47. Study the given chart carefully. Which of the following correctly identifies X, Y and Z? **(2018)**

	X	Y	Z
(a)	Ostrich	Housefly	Whale
(b)	Butterfly	Spider	octopus
(c)	Penguin	Bedbug	Shark
(d)	Ostrich	Emu	Duck

X
It has feathers but it cannot fly.
Y
It has six legs but it can fly.
Living things
Z
It has no legs but it can swim.

48. Select the option which correctly fills the blank in the use given riddle. **(2018)**

I eat green grass and I look like horse. I have black and white stripes all over. I kick very hard and you can't tame me. My baby is known as _____.

(a) Cub (b) Joey (c) Foal (d) Calf

49. Unscramble the given letters to find the names of animal homes and then select the correct match of the animal and its home. **(2019)**

(a)  - BEW (b)  - DHES

(c)  - ETABLES (d)  - POOC

50. Select the set-up in which if a rabbit is put, it will live for the shortest time. **(2019)**

(a) 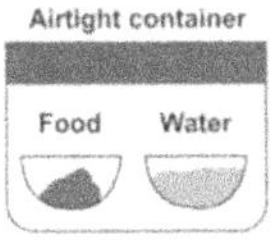 Airtight container
Food Water

(b) 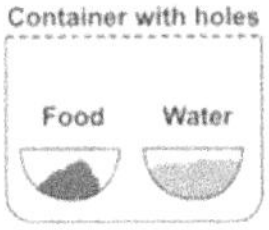 Container with holes
Food Water

(c) 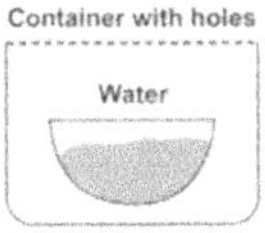 Container with holes
Water

(d) 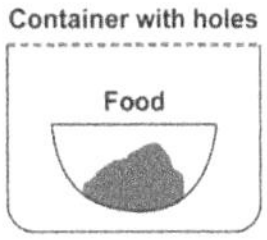 Container with holes
Food

51. Riya made four groups of animals that eat plants only but in one of the groups, she mistakenly placed one animal that eats both plants and animals. Identity this group and select the correct option. (2019)

(a) Giraffe, Elephant, Horse
(b) Rabbit, Sheep, Goat
(c) Zebra, Yak Buffalo
(d) Bear, Cow, Deer

52. Study the given word-chop table. Which of the following sets of boxes will give the name of an animal that lives in a hole? (2021)

1 BE	2 SP	3 SNA	4 LI
5 HOR	6 AR	7 ON	8 ID
9 DE	10 KE	11 SE	12 ER

(a) 4 and 7
(b) 5 and 11
(c) 3 and 10
(d) 2, 8 and 12

53. In the given table, few animals are classified into two groups P and Q, on a certain basis. Select the option that correctly identifies P and Q. (2021)

Group P	Group Q
Whale	Monkey
Fish	Giraffe
Octopus	Bear
Dolphin	Buffalo

	P	Q
(a)	Farm animals	Wild animals
(b)	Big animals	Small animals
(c)	Wild animals	Domestic animals
(d)	Water animals	Land animals

54. Select the correct statement. (2022)

(a) Blue whale is the largest animal in the world.
(b) Elephant is the tallest animal on land.
(c) Giraffe is the largest animal on land.
(d) Zebra is called the 'ship of the desert'.

55. Match column I with column II and select the correct option. (2022)

Column-I	Column II
(A) Wild animal	(1) Cow
(B) Bird	(2) Dog
(C) Pet animal	(3) Butterfly
(D) Farm animal	(iv) Lion
(E) Insect	(5) Eagle

(a) A-3, B-4, C-1, D-2, E-5
(b) A-2, B-1, C-3, D-4, E-5
(c) A-4, B-5, C-2, D-1, E-3
(d) A-2, B-3, C-1, D-4, E-5

56. Match the following: **(2022)**

Column A		Column B
1.		A Beak
2.		B Fins
3.	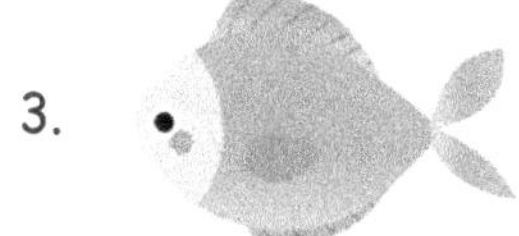	C Six legs
4.		D Sticky tongue

(a) 1 → C, 2 → B, 3 → D, 4 → A

(b) 1 → C, 2 → D, 3 → B, 4 → A

(c) 1 → D, 2 → C, 3 → A, 4 → B

(d) 1 → C, 2 → A, 3 → B, 4 → D

57. Which combination of statements is correct regarding the animal shown below? **(2022)**

1. **It is a lion.**
2. **It lives in the forest.**
3. **It eats the flesh of other animals.**
4. **It hunts deers for its food.**

(a) Only 1 and 2 (b) Only 2 and 4

(c) Only 2, 3 and 4 (d) All 1, 2, 3 and 4

RESPONSE GRID

LEVEL 1

1. a b c d	2. a b c d	3. a b c d	4. a b c d	5. a b c d
6. a b c d	7. a b c d	8. a b c d	9. a b c d	10. a b c d
11. a b c d	12. a b c d	13. a b c d	14. a b c d	15. a b c d
16. a b c d	17. a b c d	18. a b c d	19. a b c d	20. a b c d
21. a b c d	22. a b c d	23. a b c d	24. a b c d	25. a b c d
26. a b c d	27. a b c d	28. a b c d	29. a b c d	30. a b c d
31. a b c d	32. a b c d	33. a b c d	34. a b c d	35. a b c d
36. a b c d	37. a b c d	38. a b c d	39. a b c d	40. a b c d
41. a b c d	42. a b c d	43. a b c d	44. a b c d	45. a b c d
46. a b c d	47. a b c d	48. a b c d	49. a b c d	50. a b c d
51. a b c d	52. a b c d	53. a b c d	54. a b c d	55. a b c d
56. a b c d	57. a b c d	58. a b c d		

LEVEL 2

1. a b c d	2. a b c d	3. a b c d	4. a b c d	5. a b c d
6. a b c d	7. a b c d	8. a b c d	9. a b c d	10. a b c d
11. a b c d	12. a b c d	13. a b c d	14. a b c d	15. a b c d
16. a b c d	17. a b c d	18. a b c d	19. a b c d	20. a b c d
21. a b c d	22. a b c d	23. a b c d	24. a b c d	25. a b c d
26. a b c d	27. a b c d	28. a b c d	29. a b c d	30. a b c d
31. a b c d	32. a b c d	33. a b c d	34. a b c d	35. a b c d
36. a b c d	37. a b c d	38. a b c d	39. a b c d	40. a b c d
41. a b c d	42. a b c d	43. a b c d	44. a b c d	45. a b c d
46. a b c d	47. a b c d	48. a b c d	49. a b c d	50. a b c d
51. a b c d	52. a b c d	53. a b c d	54. a b c d	55. a b c d
56. a b c d	57. a b c d			

Solutions with Explanation

LEVEL 1

1. **(b)** Tiger is a wild animal. Cow, goat & hen are domestic animals.
2. **(c)** Ostrich is a bird, but it can't fly. Crow, parrot & peacock can fly.
3. **(d)** Both crocodile and frog live in water. Parrot is a bird that flies in air.
4. **(a)** Dog lives in our house and is called pet.

5. (b) We get wool from sheep.

6. (d) Horse, Donkey and Ox all are used for transportation purpose.

7. (a) Crow is a bird which lays eggs.

8. (c) Monkey lives on trees.

9. (a) Cat - Kennel, Dog lives in a kennel and cat lives in a cattery.

10. (a) Giraffe is a wild animal.

11. (b) Crocodile lives in water.

12. (d) Birds have wings and beak and it lays egg.

13. (b) All these animals are examples of wild animals.

14. (b) Parrot is a bird that can fly. Ostrich, ant and fish cannot fly..

15. (b) Tiger is the National animal of India.

16. (b) Peacock is a bird.

17. (b) Horse is a domestic animal and used for transportation.

18. (c) 19. (b) 20. (c) 21. (a)

22. (d) 23. (b) 24. (b)

25. (b) Spider has eight legs and it lives in a web. Honey bee gives us honey and it lives in a hive.

26. (d)

27. (b) Domestic animals are those animals that are kept by humans for some purpose, such as for work or food or as a pet. Sheep gives us wool and hen gives us egg and meat. Elephant and horse are used for transportation. Wild animal is an animal that lives in nature and is not cared for by humans, e.g., crocodile, zebra, kangaroo, etc.

28. (d) 29. (d)

30. (b) Birds nest in trees but owl lives in tree holes as well as in the ground holes.

31. (c) 32. (a)

33. (d) Mane are the long hair around the neck in lion. Trunk is the upper lip and nose of the elephant. Muzzle is the part of face, including nose and mouth in wolf. Whiskers are the type of hairs around nose which are not present in penguins.

34. (b) Duck (b) is a flying bird whereas penguin (a), Ostrich (c) and Kiwi (d) are flightless birds.

35. (d)

36. (c) Birds have 2 legs while insects insects have 6 legs. Spider has 8 legs thus it is not an insect.

37. (d)

38. (c) Donkey - bray
Monkey- chatter
39. (c) Earthworm
40. (d) Kennel - dog
Coop - hen
41. (c) The group of elephant is called a herd or parade
42. (b)
43. (a) Elephant
44. (c) 45. (d) 46. (c) 47. (c) 48. (d)
49. (c)
50. (d) Foal- a young horse.
51. (b)
52. (c) A group of frog is called-knot or Army
53. (b) Bats give birth to living ones.
54. (a) Frog
55. (d) Baby of elephant is called calf which is same as the baby of a cow.
56. (a) Shark
57. (a) Crow has wings
58. (b) Pattern of series-

$$7 \xrightarrow{+2} 9 \xrightarrow{+4} 13 \xrightarrow{+6} 19 \xrightarrow{+8} \textcircled{27} \xrightarrow{+10} 37$$

LEVEL 2

1. (b) Cheetah is the fastest running land animal.
2. (a) Cow gives us milk.
3. (b) Elephant is the largest land animal.
4. (c) Dog is small from lion, cheetah and elephant.
5. (d) Elephant (d) is the biggest animal on land and blue whale (f) is the biggest animal on Earth.
6. (d) The passage describes that the animals are of different kinds and are found in different places.
7. (a) A horse lives in a stable. A sty is a place where domestic pigs are kept.
8. (b) Vulture eats the flesh of dead animals.
9. (b) This is a butterfly.

10. (c) Cow is a domestic animal and gives us milk.
11. (a) Insects have six legs, four wings and zero teeth.
12. (b) forest
13. (c) Lion
14. (a) Tiger
15. (b) flesh
16. (a) Domestic
17. (b) Tortoise.
18. (d) Camel.
19. (b) feathers.
20. (a) teeth.
21. (a) Pet.
22. (c) Lion lives in Den, Dog in kennel, horse in stable, Bird in nest.
23. (c) 'Y' is frog. Frog can live in water as well as on land.
24. (b) Animals don't have feathers, Birds don't have teeth. Birds have feathers & Insects have wings.
25. (a) 6

(1) D	E	H (4)	L	I	(5) D	U	C	K
(2) E	L	E	P	H	(6) A	N	T	A
E	(3) S	N	A	K	E	M	U	W
R	A	T	U	R	K	E	Y	I

26. (b) The given word grid contains the name of 3 animals that eat animals only i.e. lion, snake and wolf, and the names of 2 animals that eat plants only i.e. cow and goat.

P	N	C	Z	M	L
L	I	O	N	V	T
S	G	W	U	B	C
N	O	B	E	A	R
A	A	M	J	Q	O
K	T	I	G	E	W
E	W	O	L	F	X

27. (b) Option (b), i.e., STABLE is the home of horse (animal shown in the picture). Option (a) is NEST, (c) is SHED and (d) is COOP.

28. (d) 29. (b)

30. (c) Ravi should stop the people who are throwing stones at animals.

31. (d) X - Dog is a pet. Y - Eagle is a bird

32. (d) Duck, fish and frog live in water.

33. (c) Monkey lives on tree.

34. (b) Frog can live in water as well as on land.

35. (c) Elephant is a wild animal.

36. (c) Total number of domestic animals = 3 (Cow, Hen, Rabbit)

Total number of Birds = 2 (Ostrich, Parrot)

Total number of water animals = 1 (Frog)

Total number of domestic animals + Total number of birds + Total number of water animals, (3 + 2 + 1) = 6

37. (d) 38. (b) 39. (d)

40. (a) 41. (d) 42. (b)

43. (b) 44. (d) 45. (c)

46. (d) Bee-hive

47. (a) Ostrich has feathers but it cannot fly-housefly has six legs and it can fly Whale has no legs but it can swim.

48. (c) Baby zebra is known as foal.

49. (d) Hen- coop

50. (a) In an air tight container, rabbit will live for shortest time.

51. (d) Bear can eat both animals as well as plants.

52. (c) Snake lives in hole.

53. (d) Group P represents water animals and group Q represents land animals .

54. (a)

55. (c) Lion is a wild animal.

56. (b) 57. (c)

4 CHAPTER FOREWORD

When your mother baked your favourite cake for your birthday, how did you know about it? Do you remember how does your favourite sweet smells or taste?

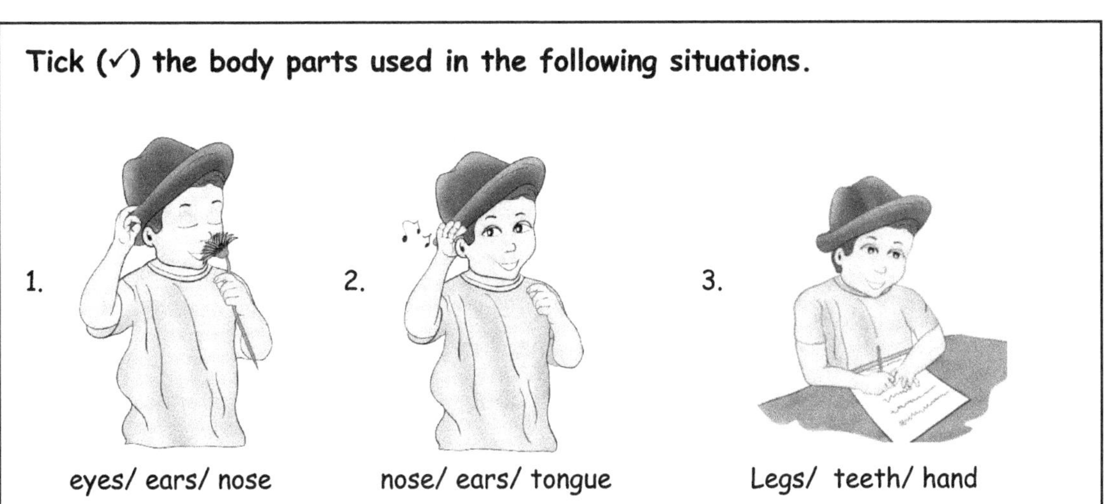

Tick (✓) the body parts used in the following situations.

1. eyes/ ears/ nose
2. nose/ ears/ tongue
3. Legs/ teeth/ hand

When you finish reading this chapter, you will be able to know more about your body and body parts, needs of your body and how to stay healthy.

4 Chapter

Human Body and Their Needs

Amazing facts

- A human eye can distinguish about 10 million different colours.

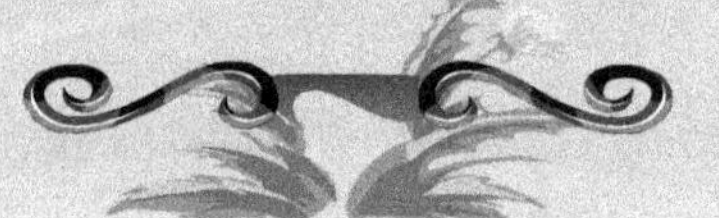

LEARNING OBJECTIVES

This lesson will help you to:

- Know about your body and its different parts.
- Study the different function of our body.
- Learn about the food items which help us to stay healthy.
- Study about the needs of human body.
- Know about different types of clothes that protect our body.

INTRODUCTION

You must have learnt about your body parts. Can you name some of them.

SENSE ORGANS

Our body is made up of different organs. These organs help us to know the world around us. These are called **Sense Organs**.

Real life examples

There are 206 bones in an adult human body. Babies at the time of birth have more than 270 bones. Some of these bones fuse together at later stages of growth and form 206 bones.

Our **tongue** helps us to taste food.

Our **eyes** help us to see things

Our **ears** help us to hear sounds.

Our **skin** helps us to feel

Our **nose** helps us to smell

Misconcept/ Concept

Misconcept: Brain is non-functional when we sleep.

Concept: Brain is active throughout the life, even when you are asleep, it is more active when you are sleeping.

Our body is made up of different parts. Some parts play a very important role and help us to live. Let us study these parts in detail.

PARTS OF OUR BODY

a) BRAIN:

Brain is present in the head of the body.

- Brain controls all the activities of our body.
- Brain gives instruction to all other parts of our body.
- All the thinking & memorising work is done by the brain.

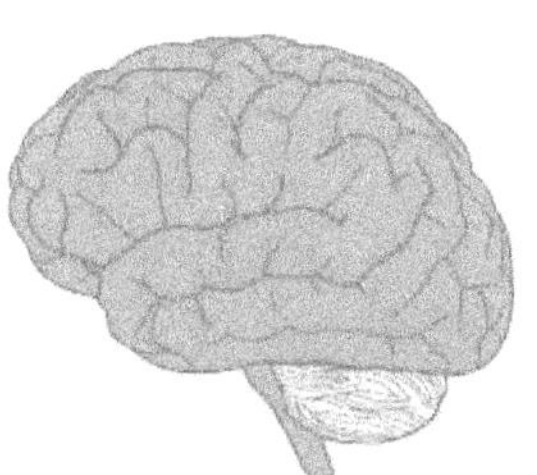

Brain

b) HEART:

Heart is present in the chest.

- It is an internal organ of our body. It supplies blood to all parts of body.
- Normally heart beat of a healthy person is 72-75 times in one minute.

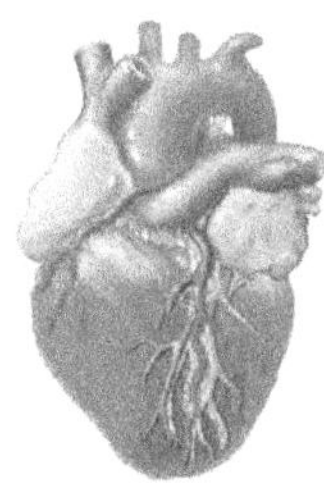

Heart

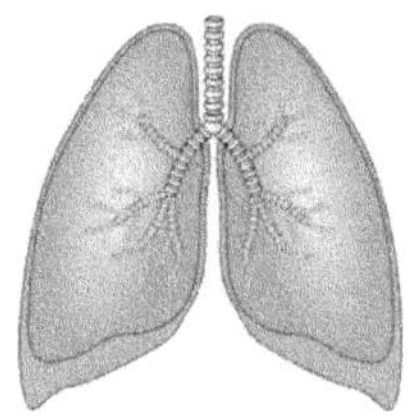

c) **LUNGS:**

- Lungs are present in the chest. Human body has two lungs.
- Lungs help in breathing & purifying the blood.

d) **ARMS:**

- Every human being has 2 arms. Each arm consists of elbow, wrist, hand and fingers.
- Hands are used for eating, writing, combing, cleaning etc.

e) **LEGS:**

- Legs are the lower part of our body.
- Human beings have 2 legs.
- Legs are used for walking, running etc.
- Legs contain thighs, knees, ankles, fingers and toes.

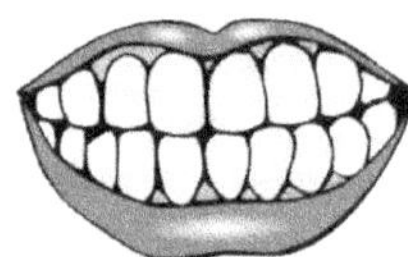

f) **TEETH:**

Teeth are very hard and are white in colour.

- Teeth lie inside the mouth.
- Teeth are used for chewing and tearing the food.
- A human body has 20 milk teeth up to the age of 6 years. An adult has 32 teeth and they are called Permanent teeth.

NEEDS OF HUMAN BODY

Our body needs some basic things to live and grow. Let us study what are the basic necessities of life.

a) **FOOD:** We need good food to grow and stay healthy.

DIFFERENT TYPES OF FOODS

- Some foods help us to GROW.

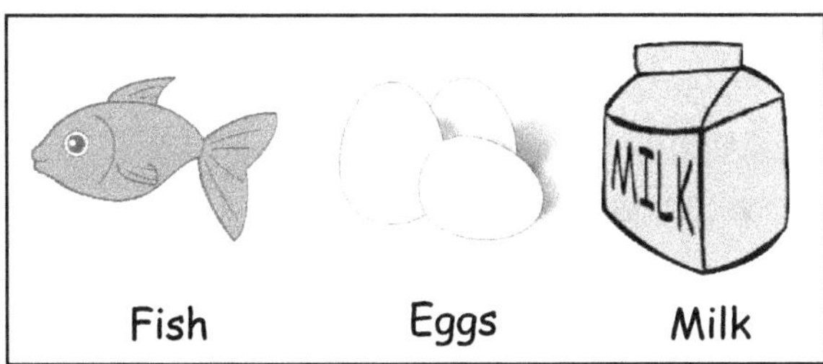

Fish Eggs Milk

- Some foods give us ENERGY to work and play.

Bread Rice Potato

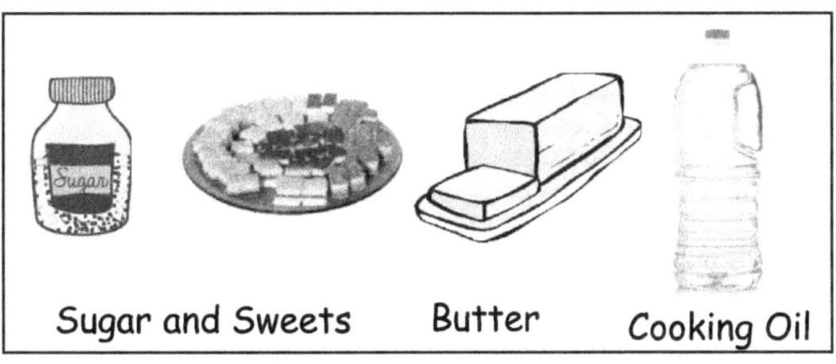

Sugar and Sweets Butter Cooking Oil

Fact Box

- ❖ Foods like Pizza, Burger, Chocolate Chowmin, Chips, etc. are called junk food. They are unhealthy and should be avoided as much as possible.
- ❖ A honey bee has 5 eyes.
- ❖ Dolphins sleep with one eye open.

- Some foods keep away diseases. They help us to remain healthy.

Fruits

Vegetables

b) **WATER:** We also need water. We should drink 6-8 glasses of water daily.

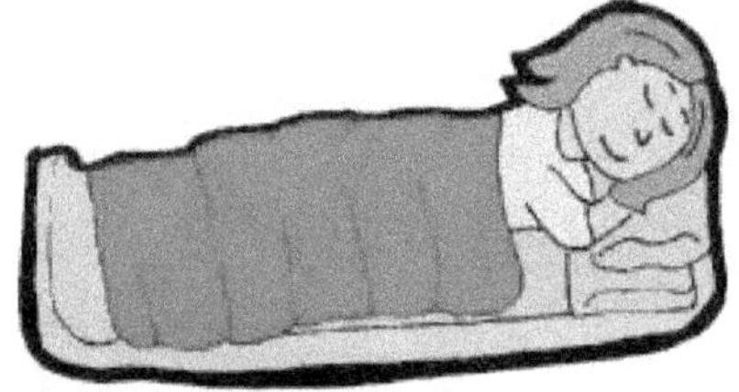

c) **REST AND EXERCISE:** We need rest or sleep. We should sleep at least eight hours a day.

- Exercise also helps us to become strong and stay healthy.
- Walking, running and swimming are good exercises. Playing is also a good exercise.

d) **CLOTHES:** We all wear colourful fancy clothes to look good. Do you know clothes protect us from heat, cold and rain.

Let us study different types of clothes that are used.

TYPES OF CLOTHES

1. **Cotton Clothes**
   - The clothes which are made from cotton are called cotton clothes.
   - They are mostly used in summer season.
   - For example: Shirts, Trousers, frocks, saree etc.

2. **Woollen Clothes:**
   - The clothes made up of wool are called woollen clothes.
   - They are mostly used in winters to keep us warm.
   - For example: Sweaters, Coat, Caps etc.

3. **Rainy Clothes:**
   - The clothes which protect us from getting wet during the rains are called rainy clothes.
   - For Eg: Raincoat, Boots.

What type of clothes do you wear when you are invited in a birthday party or in a marriage?

Occasional Clothes: Clothes which we wear on some special occasions, festivals and events are different from our daily wears.

For example: Girls wear fancy lehengas and boys wear party suits while going to a marriage.

At the time of festival, for example, on diwali we wear traditional clothes.

Did You Know?

- People wore clothing to protect themselves in battle. Medieval knights wore heavy armor and helmets. So did japanese Samurai warriors. Clothing for every day was made from natural fibres, such as cotton, linen, wool and silk. Cotton and linen fabric are made from plants, while silk is made from fibres spun from silkworms! Wool is sheared from - you guessed it - sheep. People used dyes from berries and plants to color the fabric. They didn't have zippers, buttons or Velcro, but instead, used ties.
- Scientists have used the study of lice - yes, lice - to create theories about when clothing was first developed. Body lice live in clothing and that species split off from head lice around 100,000 years ago.
- Polyester is a common material used to make clothing and it is basically a plastic.
- Sometimes men wear skirts such as togas and kilts. While that is not common in most areas today, historically they were normal day to day wear.

Multiple Choice Questions

LEVEL 1

1. Which part of our body helps us to see things?

(a) Ears (b) Teeth (c) Eyes (d) Hands

2. Which of the following part controls all the activities in our body?

(a) Eyes (b) Ears (c) Brain (d) Nose

3. Which of the following is the function of heart? [Tricky]

(a) Supply blood to our body (b) Hears sound

(c) Help in breathing (d) Helps us to feel.

4. How many lungs does a human body have?

(a) 1 (b) 2 (c) 3 (d) 4

5. How many teeth are present in an adult? [2012, Tricky]

(a) 20 (b) 30 (c) 32 (d) 64

6. Which of the following is the part of Leg?

(a) Elbow (b) Toes

(c) Knee (d) Both (b) and (c)

7. ___________ is present in the chest.

(a) Heart (b) Eye (c) Brain (d) All of these

8. How many legs does a human beings have?

(a) 4 (b) 3 (c) 2 (d) 1

9. Which part of our body helps in breathing?

(a) Heart (b) Brain

(c) Lungs (d) None of these

10. Which of the following is an example of healthy food?

(a) Fruits (b) Rice

(c) Pizza (d) both (a) and (b)

11. Which part of our body helps us to watch television?

(a) Eye (b) Skin

(c) Nose (d) Both (a) and (b)

12. Which of the following increases energy in our body? **[Tricky]**

(a) Egg (b) Fruits (c) Vegetables (d) All of these

13. Which of the following part of body helps us to know the taste of pizza.

[2013]

(a) Tongue (b) Eye

(c) Nose (d) Both (a) and (b)

14. Which of the following activities is carried out by legs?

(a) Walking (b) Eating

(c) Watching TV (d) Reading

15. Which of the following food items are unhealthy and have low nutritional value?

(a) Fruits (b) Potato Chips

(c) Chocolates (d) Both (b) and (c)

Directions (Qs. 16 to 20): Select the odd one out **[Tricky]**

16. (a) Elbow (b) Wrist (c) Hand (d) Knees

17. (a) Burger (b) Pizza (c) Apple (d) Chocolates

18. (a) Raincoat (b) Frock (c) Skirt (d) Shirt

19. (a) Eyes (b) Ears (c) Nose (d) Legs

20. (a) Eating (b) Writing (c) Combing (d) Running

21. **Which of these foods helps us to fight with illness and to stay healthy?**

(a) (b) (c) (d)

22. **Which sense organ helps you to feel hot things and cold things? [2015]**

(a) Eyes (b) Skin (c) Ear (d) Nose

23. **Helps us in ____________. [2014]**

(a) Drawing a sketch (b) Gripping the swing tightly

(c) Feeling different things (d) All of these

24. **Complete the following sentences by choosing the correct sequence of words.**

We need _____ to cover our body and a _____ to live and _____ helps us to grow and stay healthy. [2015]

(a) Clothes, Bathroom, Food (b) Leaves, House, Exercise

(c) Leaves, Kitchen, Exercise (d) Clothes, House, Food

25. **[Tricky]**

Stretched smoothly tight,
Around my body day and night ...
Largest part, That I own
Bigger than my Brain or Bone!

Which body part is being referred in the given rhyme?

(a) Stomach (b) Hand (c) Eyes (d) Skin

26. **Which of the following senses do need to realise the beauty of a butterfly ? [2015]**

(a) Smell (b) Touch (c) Taste (d) Sight

27. Nandini is listening music. Which of these she cannot sense? [Tricky]

(a) The colour of the wall in front of her

(b) The taste of the sauce

(c) Whether coffee is hot or cold

(d) None of these

28. What is correct about milk?

(a) It keeps our bones and teeth strong.
(b) We need to drink milk weekly.
(c) It is a complete meal.
(d) Both (a) and (b)

29. Select the children who will NOT be able to identify purple flower in a bunch of red flowers. [2015]

(a) 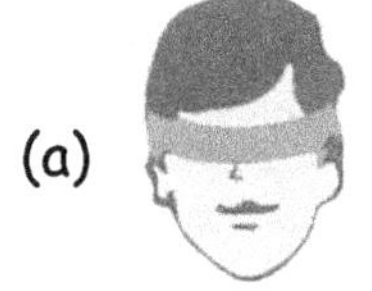
(b) 
(c) 
(d) 

30. **Madhur : Mom, it seems you have lit an incense stick (Agarbatti) in the house.**

Which body part Madhur most likely used to know about the incense stick? [2016]

(a) Ears
(b) Nose
(c) Tongue
(d) Hands

31. Select the correct match of the body part in column-I that rhymes with the word in column-II. [2015]

Column-I	Column-II
(A) Chin	1. Band
(B) Hand	2. Thin
(C) Neck	3. Close
(D) Nose	4. Check

(a) A-3, B-4, C-2, D-1
(b) A-1, B-3, C-2, D-4
(c) A-2, B-1, C-4, D-3
(d) A-1, B-2, C-3, D-4

32. **Match the column I with column II and select the correct option.** **[2014]**

	Column I		Column II
(A)		(1)	 
(B)		(2)	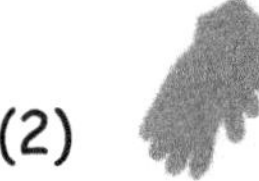
(C)		(3)	

(a) A-2, B-1, C-3 (b) A-1, B-3, C-2

(c) A-3, B-2, C-1 (d) A-1, B-2, C-3

33. **Which sense organ is the child using here ?** **[2014]**

(a) Nose

(b) Tongue

(c) Skin

(d) Ears

34. **For which part of the body is the given item used?**

(a) Eyes

(b) Nose

(c) Ear

(d) Head

35. **Match the columns and select the correct option.** **[Tricky]**

Column-I		**Column-II**
(A) Without rest	1.	To keep fit
(B) Sleep for	2.	We can fall ill
(C) Eat healthy	3.	To stay healthy
(D) Exercise helps us	4.	Eight hours everyday

(a) A-4, B-3, C-2, D-1 (b) A-2, B-4, C-3, D-1

(c) A-3, B-1, C-4, D-2 (d) A-1, B-4, C-2, D-3

36. Which sense organ is being used by the child shown in the picture? **(2019)**

(a) Nose

(b) Tongue

(c) Skin

(d) Ears

37. The words given in the box are associated with which of following sense organs? **(2018)**

Bitter, Salty, Sweet, Spicy

(a) 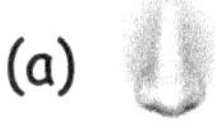 (b)  (c) 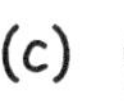   (d) 

38. For which part of the body is the given item used? **(2018)**

(a) Nose
(b) Head
(c) Ear
(d) Eye

39. On a hot sunny day, we like to **(2022)**

(a) Wear light coloured cotton clothes (b) Drink cold water
(c) Eat ice-cream (d) All of these.

40. Unscramble the given letters and select the option that gives the name of the sense organ being used by the boy in the given picture. **(2022)**

(a) EEYS (b) REAS (c) ESON (d) KISN

41. Raman is a 8 year old boy. Which among the following clothes is best for him when the whether is very hot? **(2022)**

(a)  (b) 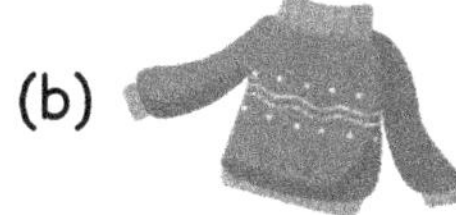 (c)   (d) 

42. Which one of the following is not an internal organ of our body? **(2022)**

(a) 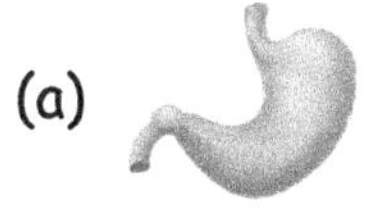 (b) 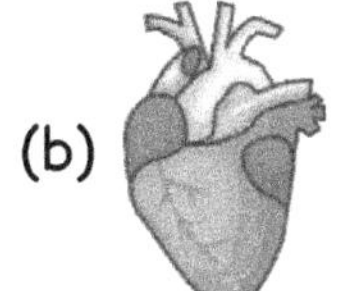 (c)  (d) 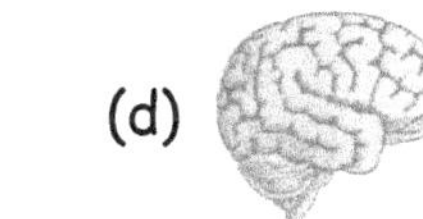

43. Which organ helps us to smell a flower? (2022)

(a) Nose (b) Eye (c) Tongue (d) Skin

LEVEL 2

1. Which of the following is used to hold things?

(a) Eye (b) Hand (c) Legs (d) Nose

2. Which of the following statements is NOT true? [2013, Tricky]

(a) Raincoat is used in rainy season.

(b) Raincoat is used in winters.

(c) Woollen cloth is used in winters.

(d) Cotton clothes are used in summers.

3. The warmth of bonfire can be help with _____. [2013]

(a) Eyes (b) Ears (c) Hands (d) Nose

4. What else can be done to keep ourselves warm on a cold day ? [2013]

(a) Wear cotton clothes (b) Drink hot milk or tea

(c) Wear woollen clothes (d) Both (b) and (c)

5. Which of the following protects us from sun in summers?

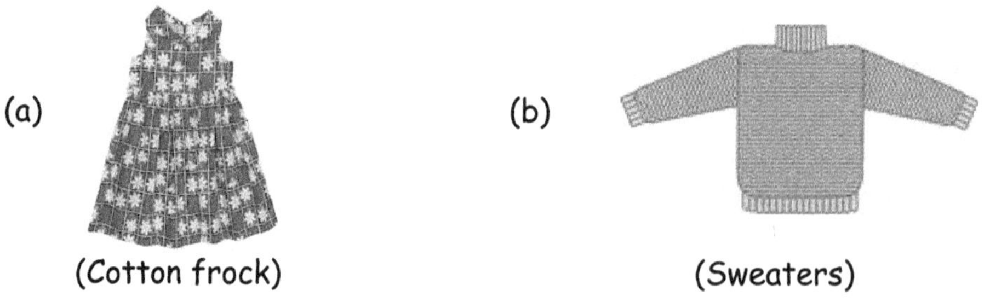

(a) (Cotton frock) (b) (Sweaters)

(c) 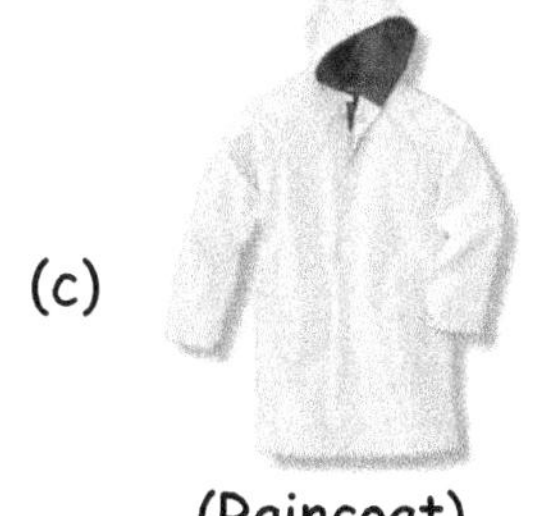

(Raincoat)

(d) All of these

6. **Starting from first letter, cross out every alternate letter. Now identify the word which is associated with sense of smell. [2013]**

(a) NBQESATUUTVIWFXUYLZ (b) SFPRQATGMRPARNACMEF

(c) LSTMNOIOVTBHA (d) VDCEDLIIOCLYOUUESA

7. **Ravi was asked to write functions (1, 2, 3 and 4) of some body parts on a picture of a boy as shown here. Which of the functions have been INCORRECTLY matched ? [2015]**

(a) 1 and 3 only (b) 1 only (c) 2 and 4 only (d) 4 only

8. **Consider the following statements and choose the correct answer.**

[Critical Thinking]

Statement A: We need good food to grow. For example: fruits and vegetables.

Statement B: Some foods help us to fight from diseases. For example: Pizza and Chocolates.

(a) Statement A is true, B is false (b) Both the statements are false

(c) Statement B is true, A is false (d) Both the statement are true

9. **Unscramble the given letters to find out which of these Rajat CANNOT sense with his closed eyes. [2015]**

(a) ORUCLO (b) EXUtter (c) osndu (c) satte

10. A group of letters is given in the box. Which of the following things needed by humans can be spelled using some of these letters? [2016]

I A L O V H C E K G M

(a) A type of summer clothing.

(b) A food that keeps our bones and teeth healthy.

(c) A room where food is cooked.

(d) A sense organ that helps us to feel objects.

11. Which of these senses is the most needed for the given activity ? [2014]

(a) Touch

(b) Smell

(c) Taste

(d) Sight

Direction (Qs. 12 to 21): Fill in the blanks in the passage given below:

Brain____(12)____all the activities in our body. Heart is present in the____(13)____. It supplies ____(14)____ to all parts of body. Human body has ____(15)____ lungs. There are 20 ____(16)____ in human body. ____(17)____ are the lowest part of human body. Legs are used for ____(18)____. ____(19)____ is unhealthy. Clothes which keep us warm in winters are called ____(20)____ clothes. ____(21)____ helps us to protect from rain. **[Critical Thinking]**

12. (a) reflects (b) controls (c) protects (d) None of these
13. (a) Brain (b) Legs (c) Chest (d) Head
14. (a) blood (b) milk (c) bread (d) fruit
15. (a) one (b) two (c) three (d) four
16. (a) eyes (b) ear (c) milk teeth (d) knees
17. (a) Brain (b) Legs (c) Hand (d) Teeth
18. (a) writing (b) walking (c) thinking (d) none of these
19. (a) Fruits (b) Milk (c) Junk Food (d) Vegetables
20. (a) cotton (b) woollen (c) rainy (d) none of these
21. (a) Raincoat (b) Sweater (c) Frock (d) Socks

22. The figure given below shows parts of a human body **[Tricky]**

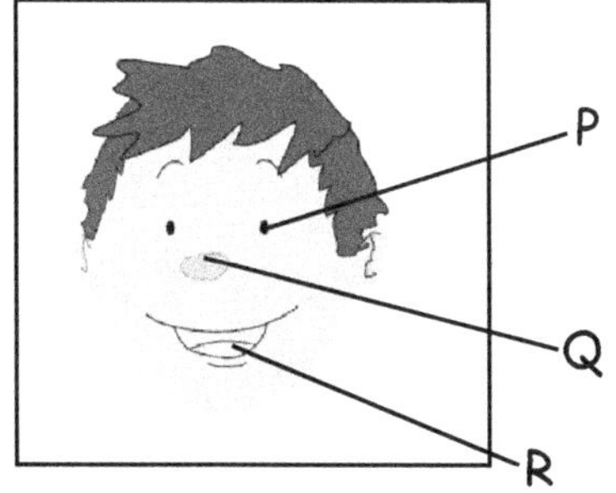

Identify the parts P, Q and R.

	P	Q	R
(a)	Nose	Tongue	Skin
(b)	Eye	Nose	Tongue
(c)	Tongue	Ear	Nose
(d)	Ear	Nose	Eye

23. Which of the following food items give us energy to do work ?

(a) Bread (b) Rice (c) Potato (d) All of these

24. Match the column (I) with column (II). **[Tricky]**

Column (I)		Column (II)	
A.	Eyes	1.	Walking
B.	Legs	2.	Loudspeaker
C.	Ears	3.	Ice cream
D.	Tongue	4.	Television

	A	B	C	D
(a)	4	3	2	1
(b)	3	4	1	2
(c)	4	1	2	3
(d)	2	3	4	1

25. Which of the following options replaces 'X' and 'Y' in the following?

Match the phrases with the given words. **[Tricky]**

Junk Food	'X'	Chocolates
Cotton clothes	Frock	'Y'

(a) X = Burger, Y = Raincoat
(b) X = Pizza, Y = Shirt
(c) X = Fruit, Y = Vegetables
(d) X = Chocolates, Y = Sweater

26. Which of the following practice is CORRECT?

(a) Wash vegetables before cooking.
(b) Wash fruits after cutting
(c) Eat fruits and vegetables daily to stay healthy
(d) Both (a) and (c)

Direction (Qs. 27 to 31): Read the passage carefully and answer the following question.

[Critical Thinking]

Clothes are very essential because it protects us from heat, cold, rain etc. Clothes are of different types. **For example** cotton clothes are used in summers season. Woollen clothes are used in winters and Rainy clothes protect us from rain. For Example Raincoat. Some clothes are used to wear in special occasions. For example: Girls use to wear fancy lehengas in marriages.

27. Clothes protect us from _______.

(a) heat
(b) plants
(c) rain
(d) both (a) & (c)

28. We wear this type of clothes in summer

(a) Cotton
(b) Woollen
(c) Raincoat
(d) All of these

29. Woollen clothes are useful to us because they protect us from ________.

(a) heat
(b) cold
(c) rain
(d) fire

30. Umbrella protects us from which of the following?

(a) Sun
(b) Rain
(c) Cold
(d) Both (a) and (b)

31. **Which of the following are occassional clothes?**

(a) Cap (b) Sweater (c) Lehenga (d) All of these

32. **Given figure shows parts of a human body. Level the parts P, Q and R.** **[Tricky]**

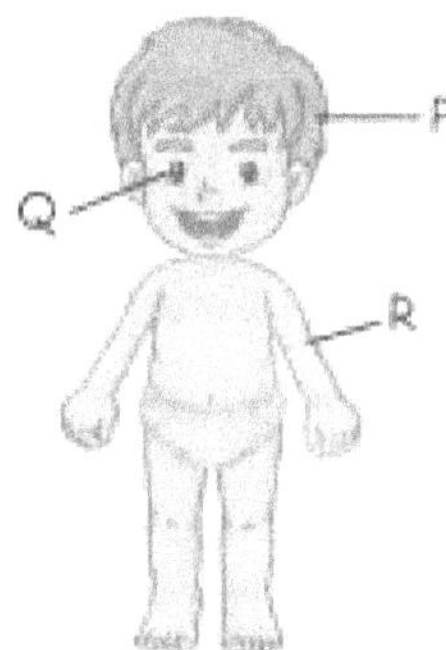

	P	Q	R
(a)	Head	Eye	Arm
(b)	Head	Nose	Leg
(c)	Neck	Ear	Foot
(d)	Neck	Cheek	Hand

33. **Which of the following statements is INCORRECT?**

(a) We get wool from plants.

(b) We should wash fruits and vegetables before eating them.

(c) We should wake up early in the morning.

(d) Our tongue helps us to taste things.

34. **Match the things given in column I with column II.** **[Tricky]**

Column I	Column II
(A) Gloves	(1) Neck
(B) Cap	(2) Hands
(C) Tie	(3) Head
(D) Shoes	(4) Foot

(a) A - 2, B - 3, C - 1, D - 4

(b) A - 2, B - 3, C - 4, D - 1

(c) A - 3, B - 2, C - 1, D - 4

(d) A - 3, B - 2, C - 4, D - 1

35. **The given figures shows that ____________.** **[Tricky]**

(a) Our skin helps us to feel things

(b) Our hand helps us to hold things

(c) We cannot lift the pot with a single hand

(d) All things are light weight except the gunny bag

36. Which of the following statements is correct? **[Tricky]**

(a) Our neck moves our head in all directions

(b) We wear woollen clothes in summer.

(c) We eat our meals in the dining room.

(d) We should not walk upright.

37. The boy shown here CANNOT identify **(2019)**

(a) Soft and hard objects

(b) Different fragrances

(c) A strawberry and vanilla ice-crream

(d) White and pink flowers.

38. Choose the correct option with respect to the given figures. **(2022)**

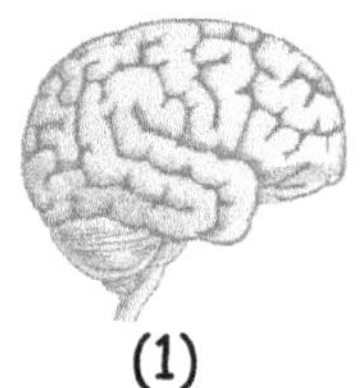

(1)

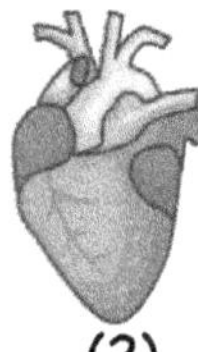

(2)

(a) Organ 1 is located in our head part while organ 2 is located in our chest part of the body.

(b) Organ 1 is located in our chest part while organ 2 is located in our head part of the body.

(c) Organ 1 is located in our head part while organ 2 is located in our abdomen part of the body.

(d) Organ 1 is located in our abdomen part while organ 2 is located in our chest part of the body.

RESPONSE GRID

LEVEL 1

1. a b c d	2. a b c d	3. a b c d	4. a b c d	5. a b c d
6. a b c d	7. a b c d	8. a b c d	9. a b c d	10. a b c d
11. a b c d	12. a b c d	13. a b c d	14. a b c d	15. a b c d
16. a b c d	17. a b c d	18. a b c d	19. a b c d	20. a b c d
21. a b c d	22. a b c d	23. a b c d	24. a b c d	25. a b c d
26. a b c d	27. a b c d	28. a b c d	29. a b c d	30. a b c d
31. a b c d	32. a b c d	33. a b c d	34. a b c d	35. a b c d
36. a b c d	37. a b c d	38. a b c d	39. a b c d	40. a b c d
41. a b c d	42. a b c d	43. a b c d		

LEVEL 2

1. a b c d	2. a b c d	3. a b c d	4. a b c d	5. a b c d
6. a b c d	7. a b c d	8. a b c d	9. a b c d	10. a b c d
11. a b c d	12. a b c d	13. a b c d	14. a b c d	15. a b c d
16. a b c d	17. a b c d	18. a b c d	19. a b c d	20. a b c d
21. a b c d	22. a b c d	23. a b c d	24. a b c d	25. a b c d
26. a b c d	27. a b c d	28. a b c d	29. a b c d	30. a b c d
31. a b c d	32. a b c d	33. a b c d	34. a b c d	35. a b c d
36. a b c d	37. a b c d	38. a b c d		

Solutions with Explanation

LEVEL- 1

1. **(c)** Eyes help us to see things.
2. **(c)** Brain controls all the activities in our body.
3. **(a)** Heart supplies blood to all parts of our body.
4. **(b)** Human body has 2 lungs.
5. **(c)** The total number of teeth in an adult is 32.
6. **(d)** both toes and knees are the part of leg. Elbow is the part of arm.
7. **(a)** Heart is present in the chest.
8. **(c)** Human beings have 2 legs.

9. (c) Lungs help in breathing, Brain helps in thinking and heart supplies blood to all parts of body.

10. (d) Fruits and Rice are healthy food. Pizza is a junk food.

11. (a) Eyes help to watch television. Nose help to smell & skin helps in feeling.

12. (a) Egg gives us energy to work and play. Fruit and vegetables keep away diseases.

13. (a) Tongue helps us to know the taste of pizza.

14. (a) Walking

15. (d) Potato Chips and chocolates both are junk food. Both are unhealthy and have low nutritional value.

16. (d) Elbow, wrist and hand are the part of arm and knees are the part of legs.

17. (c) All other are junk food. Apple is a healthy food.

18. (a) Raincoat is a cloth which we wear during rainy season.

19. (d) Eyes, ears and nose are present on the face and legs help in walking.

20. (d) Eating, writing, combing is done with the help of hands but running is done with the help of legs.

21. (c)

22. (b) The given organs are all sense organs. Skin helps us to feel hot and cold things whereas, eyes help us in seeing things. Ear helps in hearing sounds and nose helps us in smelling.

23. (d)

24. (d) We need clothes to cover our body. House is a place where we live. Food helps us to grow and stay healthy.

25. (d)

26. (d) We taste, see, smell, hear and feel with our sense organs. We can see the beautiful colour of the butterfly with our eyes.

27. (d) 28. (d)

29. (a) In the option 'A', child's eyes are closed, so he will not able to identify the purple flower in a bunch of red flower.

30. (b) Nose helps us in smelling

31. (c)

32. (d) We need raincoat, when it rains. Raincoat prevents our body from getting wet. Gloves keep our hands warm in winters. Shades (googgles) protect our eyes from the strong light of the Sun in summers.

33. (c) Child is using his hand (skin) to feel that something sticky is on his head.

34. (a) **35. (b)**

36. (c) Skin

37. (d) bitter, salty, sweet and spicy taste is felt by tongue.

38. (d) eye

39. (d) On a hoot sunny day, we like to wear light coloured cotton clothes, we drink cold water and eat ice cream.

40. (b) EARS

41. (c) **42. (c)** **43. (a)**

LEVEL- 2

1. **(b)** Hands help us to hold things.

2. **(b)** Raincoat is NOT used in winters.

3. **(c)** The warmth of bonfire can be felt with skin such as that of hands.

4. **(d)** By drinking hot milk or tea and by wearing woollen clothes, we can keep ourselves warm in a cold day.

5. **(a)** Cotton frock or cotton clothes protect us from sun in summers.

6. **(b)** ~~S~~F~~P~~R~~Q~~A~~T~~G~~M~~R~~P~~A~~R~~N~~A~~C~~M~~E~~F~~

   The word obtained from option B is FRAGRANCE, which is associated with the sense of smell.

   Option A gives BEUTIFUL (sinse of sight), option C gives SMOOTH (sense of touch) and option D gives DELICIOUS (sense of taste).

7. **(d)** In the given figure '1' is skin, which is used to feel the texture, shape, etc. of things, '2' is foot which is used for running or walking, '3' is eye with which we see things and identify colours, '4' is nose, which is used smell things.

8. **(b)** Both the statements A and B are false. Food helps us to grow and keeps us

healthy. Fruits and vegetables help us to fight against diseases.

9. (a) The unscrambled words are 'Colour' for 'ORUCLO', Texture for 'EXUTTER', sound for 'OSNDU' and Taste for 'SATTE'. Rajat's eyes are closed so he will not able to see the colour.

10. (b) Milk is the food that keeps our bones and teeth healthy.

11. (d) As the lady is ironing a dress, so the most needed sense is that of sight.

12. (b) controls
13. (c) chest

14. (a) Blood
15. (b) two

16. (c) milk teeth
17. (b) Legs

18. (b) Walking
19. (c) Junk food.

20. (b) Woollen
21. (a) Raincoat

22. (b) In the given diagram, 'P' represents, eye, 'Q' represents nose and 'R' represents tongue.

23. (d) Bread, apple and potato, all these food items give us energy to do work.

24. (c) Eyes help in watching television. Legs help in walking. Ears are used to listen the noise of loudspeaker. Tongue is used to get the taste of ice cream.

25. (b) 'X' = pizza is a junk food. 'Y' = shirt is a cotton cloth.

26. (d) We should wash vegetables before cooking and eat fruits & vegetables daily.

27. (d) Clothes protect us from heat and rain.

28. (a) Cotton clothes are used in summer.

29. (b) Woollen clothes are useful to us because they protect us from cold.

30. (d) Umbrella protects us from sun and rain.

31. (c) Lehenga is an occasional cloth.

32. (a)
33. (a)

34. (a) A - 2, B - 3, C - 1, D - 4

35. (b)
36. (c)

37. (d) The boy cannot identify white and pink flowers as he cannot see.

38. (a)

5 CHAPTER FOREWORD

Your parents must have told you not to leave their hands while walking on the road. What do you say when someone gives you a gift?

Tick(✓) for the statements which you should do and are good habits.	
1. Play on empty roads.	☐
2. Hold hands of parents when walking on the road.	☐
3. Saying please when asking for something from someone.	☐
4. Playing with food.	☐
5. Getting up late in the morning	☐

After reading this chapter, you will learn more good habits that you should follow. You will also know about safety rules and first- aid.

5
Chapter

Good Habits, Safety and First Aid

Did You Know?

- Most of the accidents take place because of breaking the traffic rules and signals.

LEARNING OBJECTIVES

This lesson will help you to:

- Learn good habits
- Know about the safety measures to be taken during work and play.
- Learn about the first aid methods to help others

Interesting facts about Exercise

- Exercising improves brain performance.
- Working out sharpen our memory.
- Have stronger muscles and bones.
- feel less tired.
- Increases energy and improve productivity of our work.

INTRODUCTION

You must have heard a well known saying that "Early to bed and early to rise makes a man healthy, wealthy and wise". This means going to bed early and getting up early in the morning is a good habit which gives us good health, money and makes us wiser. Each one of us have some habits which may be good or bad.

Let us study about some good habits in detail.

GOOD HABITS

1. To be fit we must keep our body clean.

2. We must have breakfast every morning.

3. We must brush our teeth and comb our hair.

4. We must tidy up our bedroom everyday.

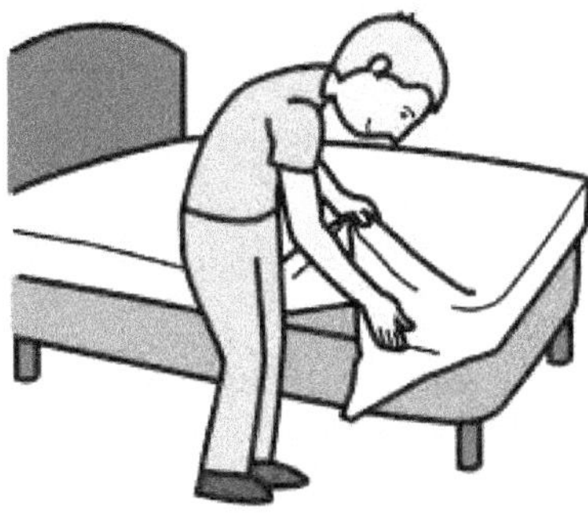

5. We must do exercise regularly to keep our body fit.

Misconcept/Concept

- Misconcept: Throw water during short circuit.
- Concept: Never throw water on the electric switches. Use sand instead of water.

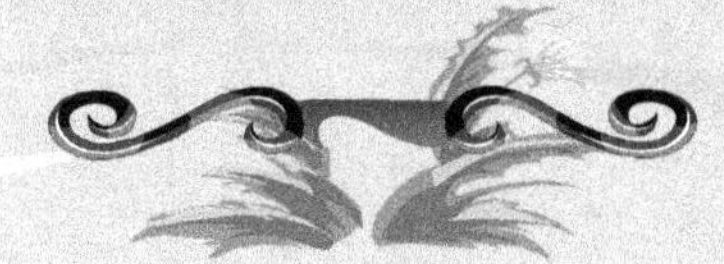

Points to remember

Always look for signals and use the pedestrian crossing to cross the road. In the absence of such markings, here is what you should do:

- Look to your right and then to the left to see if there are any approaching vehicles.
- If yes, wait for the vehicle to pass and then cross the road.
- Never cross at bends.
- Never cross between stationary vehicles.
- Adults should always accompany children aged less than six and hold their hand when crossing the street.

Historical Preview

- The first traffic light was invented by **J.P. Knight** on 9th December 1968. The first traffic light was set up in **London**.

Tips to keep a child safe on roads

Besides teaching about road safety rules for kids, parents should also keep in mind the following tips to ensure that their children stay safe on the road.

- Buckle up - Ensure that your child always wears the seat belt, or is secured in a car seat.
- Use the child lock feature to prevent your kids from opening car doors by themselves.
- Teach them about the rules practically - take them for walks and cycling, and teach them how to do it right.
- Have patience when driving - set an example for your kids to be calm and not to rush on the road.
- Be punctual and disciplined to avoid speeding and rash driving.
- Do not use mobile phones or other gadgets while driving.
- Never leave your kids alone in the car.

6. We must wash our hands before and after every meal.

7. Throw waste in Dustbin.

8. We must wash our hands after going to toilet.

Apart from these, we should also respect our elders.

Have you noticed that your parents greet their elders by touching their feet and joining their hands.

These are also good habits.

⇒ We should always wish our elders and teachers. For example: We should say '**Good Morning**' to our teachers.

⇒ Say 'Thank You' when we get something and '**Please**' when we want something.

⇒ We should always say '**Sorry**' if we hurt someone.

SAFETY

'Safety' means to keep yourself protected from harm or accident.

Your parents always tell you to be careful while walking on the road, not to run on the road, cross the road very carefully. All these are safety rules. Let us discuss these rules in detail.

1. While walking on the road always walk on the footpath. While crossing the road use the zebra crossing. Always walk on the left side of road.

2. When you travel by a bus always stand in a line. Don't get into or get off from a moving bus.
3. Do not play games on the road. Always play in the open playground.

Real Life Examples

❖ A person giving first aid to the patient

❖ Use Zebra crossing while crossing the road

Did You Know?

❖ Vulnerable road users like pedestrians, cyclists, and bikers account for around 50% of deaths due to road accidents.

❖ Wearing quality helmets reduces the chance of injury and death due to crash by 40%.

❖ Reducing or controlling the speed can reduce the chances of an injury during an accident.

❖ Child and infant car seats can decrease the number of children dying in road accidents by 54 to 80%. Making child restraint mandatory in vehicles can decrease child deaths by 35%.

❖ The chances of death by accident can be decreased by 51% with the proper use of seat belt.

❖ For every 1km/h that you reduce your speed by, you mitigate the risk of accident by 2%.

4. Obey the traffic rules. 'Stop' when the light is red and 'go' when it is green.

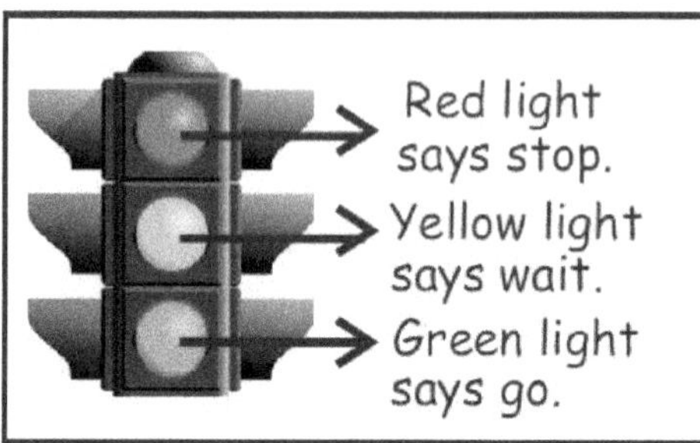

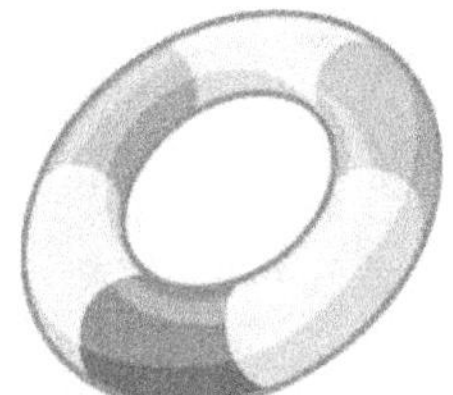

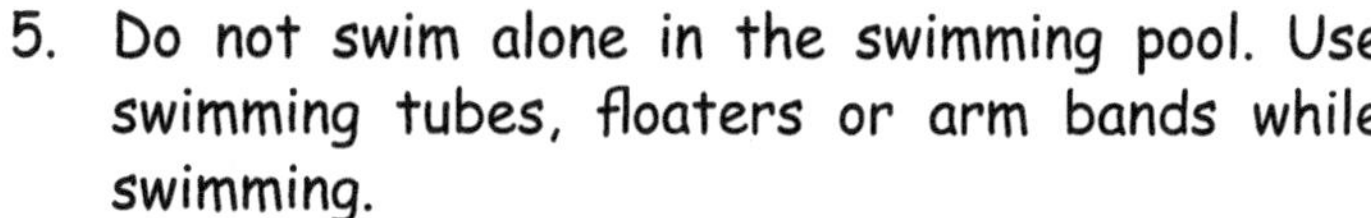

5. Do not swim alone in the swimming pool. Use swimming tubes, floaters or arm bands while swimming.

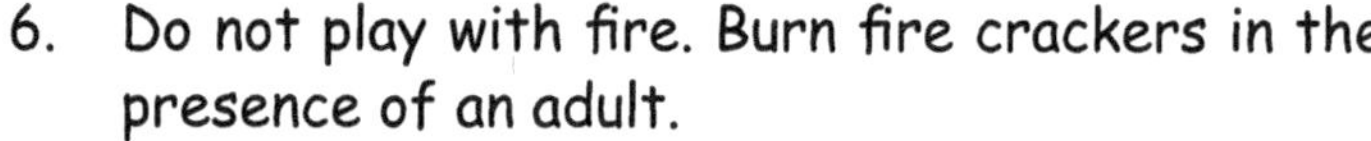

6. Do not play with fire. Burn fire crackers in the presence of an adult.

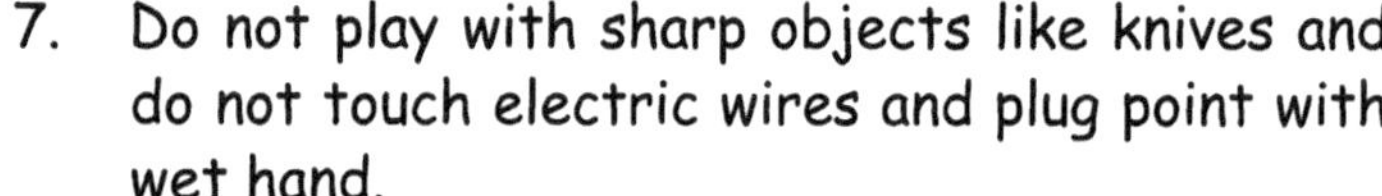

7. Do not play with sharp objects like knives and do not touch electric wires and plug point with wet hand.

FIRST AID

First aid is the first medical help given to the injured or sick person before the doctor arrives.

Multiple Choice Questions

LEVEL- 1

1. **We must exercise**

   (a) Once a month (b) Once a year (c) Daily (d) Once a week

2. **To cut our nails, we use ___________** **[2012]**

   (a) Comb (b) Soap (c) Nail cutter (d) Tooth brush

3. **A good posture helps us to stay healthy. Which of the following postures do you think is correct?** **[Tricky]**

   (a)  (b) 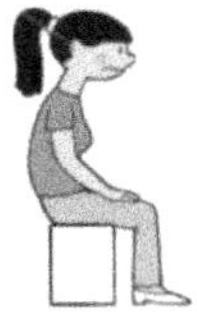 (c)  (d) All of these

4. **To wash our body, we use___________.**

   (a) 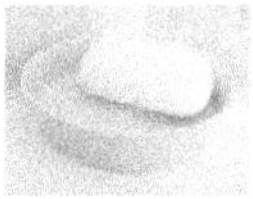 (Soap) (b)  (Comb) (c)  (Nail cutter) (d) 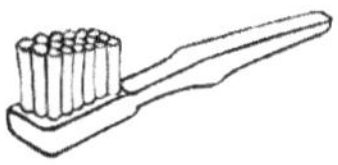 (Tooth brush)

5. **We use ___________ to clean our teeth.**

   (a)  (Soap) (b)  (Nail cutter) (c)  (Comb) (d) 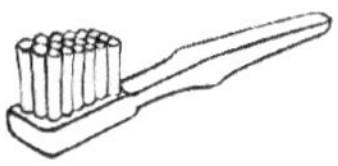 (Tooth brush)

6. **When do you brush your teeth?** **[2013]**

   (a) After I wake up (b) After playing

   (c) When I take a bath (d) After exercise

7. **Which of the following things will prevent germs on our hands from getting into our mouth?** **[2016]**

   (a)  (b)

   (c)  (d)

8. **Always cover your mouth with your hands when you are __________.**
   (a) Sneezing (b) Coughing
   (c) Yawning (d) All of these
9. **You must walk on me when you cross the road. I am a __________ crossing.** **[Tricky]**
   (a) footpath (b) traffic (c) zebra (d) horse
10. **Which of the following is a good habit?**
    (a) Respect your elders.
    (b) Brush your teeth.
    (c) Use zebra crossing to cross the road.
    (d) All of these
11. **Identify the picture that is following safety rules while travelling in a bus.** **[Tricky]**

    (a) Getting into the bus in a line.  (b) putting hands out of the vehicle

    (c) moving out of running bus  (d) Disturbing the driver while driving
12. **Which of the following safety rules should be followed in the swimming pool?** **[Tricky]**
    (a) Swim alone in the swimming pool.
    (b) Push or pull each other into the water.
    (c) Go to the deep side of the pool.
    (d) Use swimming tubes, floaters or arm bands.
13. **Which child may get an electric shock?** **[2015]**

    (a)  (b)

    (c)  (d)

14. Which of the following activities shown in picture is NOT safe? [Tricky]

(a) 

(b) 

(c) 

(d) All of these

15. _____ is the immediate help given to a person who is injured, before doctor arrives [2014]

(a) Critical Aid
(b) First Aid
(c) Medical Treatment
(d) All of these

16. Who among the following children is/are obeying safety rules ? [2015]

(a) 

(b) 

(c) 

(d) 

17. Consider the following statement and choose the correct answer. [Tricky]

Statement A: We should take bath every night.

Statement B: We should say sorry if we hurt someone.

(a) Statement A is true, Statement B is false.
(b) Statement B is true, Statement A is false.
(c) Both the statements are true.
(d) Both the statements are false.

18. What is X and Y in the given rhyme on traffic signal? [Tricky]

"... X..." light, "...Y..."
light, what do you say? "I say
get ready to go and go
right away"

	X	Y
(a)	Red	Yellow
(b)	Yellow	Green
(c)	Green	Green
(d)	Red	Red

19. Which of these safety rules is INCORRECT ? **[2013]**

(a) Never play in a playground
(b) Never go swimming alone
(c) Never run after a moving bus.
(d) Never cross the road when traffic light is green for vehicles.

20. ________ when the traffic light is red and ________ when it is green.

(a) Go, stop (b) Stop, go (c) Walk, go (d) Go, walk

21. Which of the following activities should we do twice a day? **[2015]**

(a) **(b)** **(c)** **(d)**

22. How can you put the given things in a group? **[Tricky]**

(a) Things with sharp edges
(b) Things that can cut your hand
(c) Things that can hurt you
(d) Things that can burn your fingers

23. Identify the child among the following who is NOT following safety rule. **[2015]**

(a) 

(b) 

(c) 

(d) All of these

24. Which amongst these children has the correct posture? [2014]

(a) 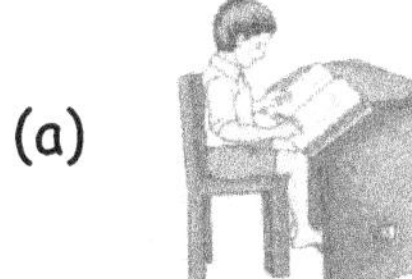 (b)  (c)  (d) 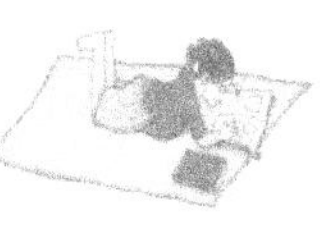

25. Amrita : I use clean hanky to blow my nose. **[2017, Tricky]**

Jaya : I splash my eyes with soap water many times a day to freshen my eyes.

Sidharth : I clean my ears with toothpick.

Which child has developed unsafe habit for cleaning the body?

(a) Amrita (b) Sidharth

(c) Jaya and Sidharth (d) Amrita, Jaya and Sidharth

26. Mohit throws things here and there in the house. This will _______.

(a) Help him to find things easily

(b) Make him or someone else trip on things

(c) Help him to clean his house

(d) None of these

27. Look at the picture and complete the following paragraph by choosing the correct sequence of words. [Critical Thinking]

We must keep our house clean

Manjeet is keeping the _________ in their right place. Saurabh is throwing the waste into the _________. Simran has finished playing. She is now keeping the _________ in the box. Latika is worried because Aman is _________ on the wall.

(a) Toys, box, books, painting.
(b) Books, dustbin, toys, drawing
(c) Eatables, almirah, toys, painting
(d) Waste, cup, toys, drawing

28. Which of the following children you should NOT follow ? [2015]

(a)  **(b)** **(c)**  **(d)** 

29. On footpath always walk _____. [2013]

(a) On your left side
(b) On your right side
(c) Anywhere you want
(d) Cannot say

30. Which of these should NOT be done for the situation as shown in the picture? [2016]

(a) Wait for the bus to stop to get in
(b) Make a queue while getting into the bus
(c) Run after the moving bus
(d) All of these

31. Which of the following activity we should do everyday?

(a) Breakfast (b) Bathing (c) Brushing (d) All of these

32. Which of these you should NOT do while eating? (2018)

(a) Chew food with mouth closed
(b) Chew food slowly
(c) Avoid talking
(d) Stuff your mouth with food

33. The conversion among three friends is given as follow? (2019)
Who among these children show good habits?

(a) Sneha and Neetu
(b) Sneha and Rohan
(c) Rohan and Neetu
(d) Sneha, Rohan and Neetu

34. Which of the following should we do? (2019)

1 2 3 4 5

(a) 2, 4 and 5 only
(b) 2, 3 and 5 only
(c) 1, 4 and 5 only
(d) 1, 3 and 4 only

35. Which of these is correct? (2019)

	Do's	**Don'ts**
(a)	Respect your elders	Eat healthy meals
(b)	Follow the traffic rules	Play with fire
(c)	Wear seats belt in the car	Wash your hands before eating
(d)	Both B and C	

36. Refer to the given figure showing road safety rules. How many of these safety rules should we follow? (2019)

(a) Two
(b) Three
(c) One
(d) Five

37. Read the given passage. (2020)

You can get an electric __p__ if you touch plug points with wet hands. Do not play with knives and blades. You can get a __q__.

Select the correct option to complete the passage.

	p	q
A.	Shock	Cut
B.	Burn	Fracture
C.	Bite	Burn
D.	Shock	Bite

38. Refer to the given picture of Aman. Aman should go to the ______. (2020)

(a) Bank

(b) Post office

(c) Hospital

(d) Library

39. Select the option which on unscrambling, gives the name of an object that should be worn while doing the activity shown in the given picture. (2021)

(a) EASTLEBT

(b) HMETEL

(c) VOGELS

(d) FCASR

40. Which of the following road signs shows school ahead? (2021)

(a) 

(b) 

(c) 

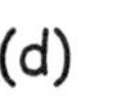

(d) 

41. Which of the following shows a good habit? (2022)

(a) 

(b) 

(c) 

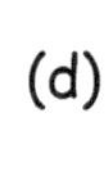

(d) 

42. Select the road sign that represents 'No Honking'. (2022)

(a) 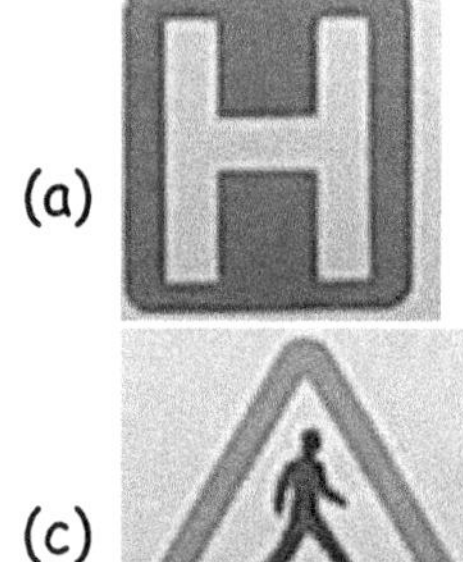

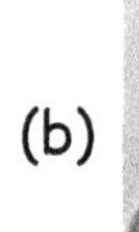

(b) 

(c)

(d) 

43. Children should not play with which of the following things of our body? (2022)

(a)  (b)  (c) 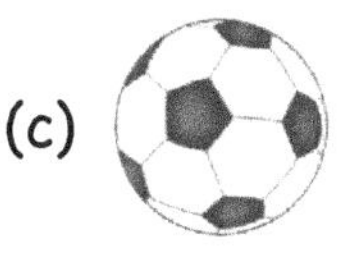 (d) 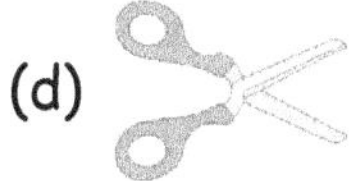

LEVEL- 2

Direction (Qs. 1 to 6): Fill in the blanks in the passage given below.

We should keep our body clean. We must take _____(1)_____ every morning. We should wash our hands before and after every _____(2)_____. We should do _____(3)_____ daily which keeps our _____(4)_____ strong. We should eat_____(5)_____ food to stay _____(6)_____. **[Critical Thinking]**

1. (a) breakfast (b) lunch
(c) dinner (d) All of these

2. (a) night (b) meal
(c) bath (d) study

3. (a) bath (b) exercise
(c) study (d) dinner

4. (a) bones (b) teeth
(c) sleep (d) both(a) & (c)

5. (a) breakfast (b) good
(c) bad (d) dinner

6. (a) healthy (b) wealthy
(c) wise (d) None of these

7. Match the Column - I with Column - II and select the correct option.

Column - I		Column - II	
A.	Without Rest	1.	fall ill
B.	Sleep	2.	stay healthy
C.	Eat healthy	3.	8 hours daily
D.	Exercise	4.	help us to keep fit

	A	B	C	D
(a)	3	4	2	1
(b)	1	3	2	4
(c)	2	1	4	3

(d) 1 2 3 4

8. **Which of the following statements is INCORRECT?** **[2013]**
   (a) Use your hanky when you are suffering from cough.
   (b) Always bite your nails.
   (c) Turn off the tap after washing your hands.
   (d) Throw garbage into the dustbin.

9. **Select the correct match of the habit and the place where it should be practised.** **[2016]**

	Habit	Place		Habit	Place
(a)	Playing football –	Classroom	(b)	Running –	Road
(c)	Walking slowly –	Stairs	(d)	Bathing –	Playground

10. **What is zebra crossing?** **[Tricky]**
   (a) It is a crossing where zebras cross the road.
   (b) It is the path where pedestrians can walk.
   (c) It is a set of painted lines on the road for safe crossing.
   (d) It is a place where vehicles can be parked.

11. **Some healthy habits are given below. An item that helps us in following one of these habits is hidden in the grid. Identify the item and related habit and select the correct option.** **[2016]**

S	T	O	O	T	H	Z	N
O	P	A	S	T	O	T	A
A	T	S	N	P	T	O	L
Q	S	H	A	M	P	O	O
P	O	O	I	L	E	T	C
T	A	A	L	H	N	H	U
O	L	P	C	P	C	B	T
O	T	M	U	A	U	R	T

   (a) Keeping our nails trimmed.
   (b) Washing hands before and after eating.
   (c) Brushing teeth twice daily.
   (d) Keeping our hair clean.

12. **Your friend gets hurt while playing. What will you do?** **[2014]**
   (a) Give some first aid to him/her.
   (b) Will take him/ her to hospital.
   (c) Call an adult to help him/her.
   (d) Both (a) and (b)

13. **The given picture shows Raman in park. Select the correct option regarding it.** **[2015]**

(a) Raman will have muscle weakness due to excess of this activity.

(b) Raman will have low stamina because of this activity

(c) Raman should do this activity only once a month.

(d) None of these

14. What should you do after you come back from the park?

(a) Drink a glass of water.

(b) Wash your hand with soap.

(c) Have a healthy snack.

(d) Watch TV.

15. The conversation among three friends is given as follows: [2015]

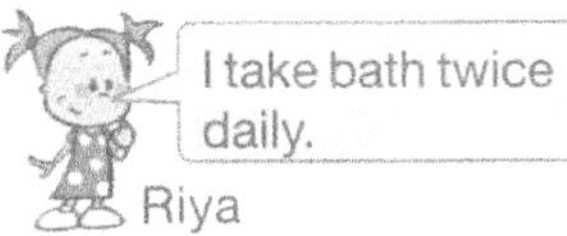

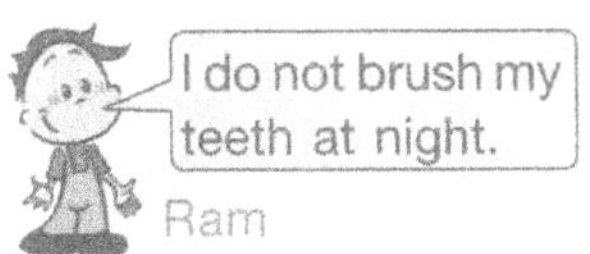

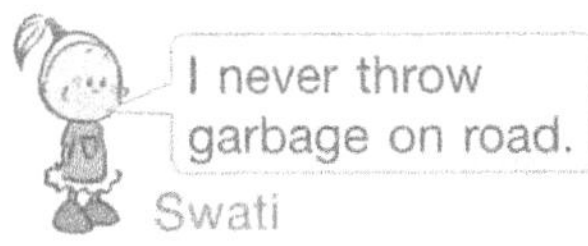

Which of these children have good habits?

(a) Swati and Ram
(b) Riya and Ram
(c) Riya and Swati
(d) Riya, Ram and Swati

16. Three activities that you should do in the morning are shown in the pictures 1, 2 and 3. [2015]

1. 

2. 

3. 

What is the corrrect order of doing these activities ?

(a) 2, 1, 3 (b) 1, 2, 3 (c) 2, 3, 1 (d) 1, 3, 2

17. Consider the following statements and choose the correct option.

Statement A. We must eat breakfast every morning. **[Critical Thinking]**

Statement B. We must brush our hair and comb our teeth daily.

(a) Statement A is true, statement B is false.

(b) Statement A is false, statement B is true.

(c) Both the statements are true.

(d) None of these.

18. Which of these is NOT necessary?

Wash your hands ________.

(a) before eating (b) after eating
(c) before going to the toilets (d) after going to the toilets

19. Rajat is walking down to his home. Which of the follwoing signals should be turned on when he can safely cross the road at a zebra crossing? [2014]

1. 2. 3. 4.

(a) 1 and 4 (b) 1 and 3 (c) 2 and 3 (d) 2 and 4

20. Which of these is an INCORRECT statement regarding safety rules? [2014]

1. Wait in a queue to get into the bus.
2. Everyone should get into the bus together at the same time.
3. Children should stand at the door of a moving bus.
4. One should not get in or get out of a moving bus.

(a) 1 and 2 (b) 2 and 3 (c) 2 and 4 (d) 1 and 3

21. Select the bad habit from the following. [Tricky]

(a) We should never touch any electric gadget with wet hands.
(b) We should wash our hands before and after eating food.
(c) We must get in or get out of a moving bus.
(d) Both (a) and (c)

22. Which of the following activities can a child do alone?

(a) Burning crackers (b) Using scissors
(c) Learning swimming (d) Playing with teddy bear

23. What is the first thing you will do when a person is injured and bleeding badly on the road? [Tricky]

(a) We should call the traffic police.
(b) We should stand around the injured person.
(c) We should call the doctor.
(d) We should give immediate medical help to the injured person before the doctor arrives.

Directions (Qs. 24 to 27): Fill in the blanks in the passage given below. [Tricky]

My mother told me ____(24)____ rules which we should always follow while walking on the road. She told me, never to____(25)____ on the road. Always walk on the ____(26)____ and use ____(27)____ crossing to cross the road.

24. (a) safety (b) beauty (c) road (d) Noneofthese

25. (a) sun (b) run (c) fun (d) eat
26. (a) road (b) footpath (c) zebra (d) traffic
27. (a) zebra (b) footpath (c) narrow (d) both (a) & (b)

28. **We should not fly kites.**
    (a) in parks (b) in school ground
    (c) in open ground (d) on the open terrcae

29. **Which of the following traffic signals indicates to stop a while and go?**
    (a) The green light (b) The yellow light
    (c) The red light (d) The blue light

30. **Which of the following is wrong?**
    (a) We should play in the middle of the road.
    (b) We should fire crackers in the middle of the road.
    (c) We should play in the playground.
    (d) both (a) and (b)

31. **Which of the following should NOT be touched with wet hands?** **[2015]**

    (a) 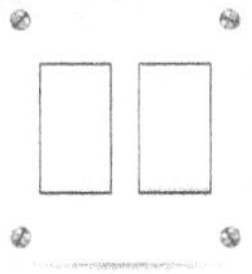 Electric Switch

    (b)  Toys

    (c) 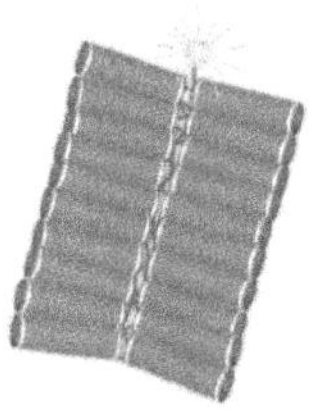 Crackers

    (d) Flowers

32. **At school, we should ____________.** **[2017]**
    (a) Never run in the corridors (b) Climb and jump on desks
    (c) Throw papers at each other (d) Push each others on swings

33. **Which of these is correct?** **[Tricky]**

	Do's	**Don't's**
(a)	Bite your nails	Lick your fingers after eating
(b)	Clean your ears with earbuds	Put finger in your nose

(c) Cover your mouth while coughing — Comb your hair daily

(d) Cut nails with nail cutter — Rinse mouth with water after eating

34. Match the columns and select the correct option.

Column-I	Column-II
(A) Cross the road at	1. Toys
(B) Always walk on the	2. Playground
(C) Play in the	3. Zebra crossing
(D) It is safe to play with the	4. Footpath

(a) A-1, B-2, C-3, D-4 (b) A-3, B-4, C-2, D-1

(c) A-4, B-3, C-1, D-2 (d) A-4, B-1, C-3, D-2

35. Which of the following statements is correct?

(a) Never flush the toilet after use

(b) Keep your books here and there after use

(c) Do not take bath everyday

(d) Wipe your shoes on the footmat before entering your house

36. We use different things to keep our house clean. Why do we use a mop? **[Tricky]**

(a) For sweeping the floor (b) For cleaning the refrigerator

(c) For dusting the furniture (d) For wiping the floor

Direction (Qs. 37 to 41): Read the following paragraph carefully and answer the following question. **[Critical Thinking]**

Our parents teach us good habits. We should always wish our elders and teachers. We should say sorry if we hurt someone. We should follow traffic rules on road. Always use footpath while walking on the road and zebra crossing while crossing the road. Never run on the road. Do not play on the road. Always play in the open playground. Do not enter in the swimming pool alone.

37. What will you do when you meet your elder?

(a) run away (b) join our hands

(c) touch their feet (d) both (b) & (c)

38. Which of the following traffic signal indicates "Go"?

(a) Red light (b) Green light

(c) Yellow light (d) None of these

39. Which of the following word will you say when you sneeze?

(a) Please (b) Thanks (c) Excuse me (d) Good night

40. Always play game in the _________.

(a) road (b) footpath

(c) playground (d) zebra crossing

41. We can enter in the _________ alone.

(a) classroom (b) road

(c) footpath (d) swimming pool

42. Select the INCORRECT option. **(2018)**

	Do's	Dont's
(a)	Eat healthy food	Eat junk food
(b)	Chew food properly	Talk while eating
(c)	Wash hands before and after eating	Eat covered food
(d)	Eat food at fixed time everyday	Skip breakfast

43. Which of the following road signs indicates 'no U turn'? **(2018)**

(a) (b) (c) (d)

44. Who among the folowlng children is/are likely to get hurt? **(2020)**

Sheena: is playing around the swimming pool
Sameer: is walking on the footpath.
Amaira: is putting her hands out of the window of a moving car.

(a) Sheena only (b) Sameer only

(c) Amaira only (d) Sheena and Amaira

Direction (Q.No. 45 and 46) : Refer to the given word grid and answer the following questions. **(2020)**

M	H	S	O	L	P	N	B
A	O	G	A	B	S	O	C
T	S	O	S	A	H	H	A
C	P	G	C	N	A	O	P
H	I	G	H	D	M	R	D
I	T	L	X	A	P	N	C
N	A	E	T	I	O	A	E
G	L	S	F	D	O	F	G
S	C	I	S	S	O	E	S
O	I	N	T	M	E	N	T

45. **Few objects are hidden in the given word grid. How many of them are found in a first aid bow? (2020)**

(a) 2 (b) 3 (c) 5 (d) 4

46. **The meaning of which of the following road side is hidden in the given word grid?? (2020)**

(c) 

(d) 

47. **Select the INCORRECT statement regarding the safety rules that we should follow while riding in a car. (2021)**

(a) We should always wear seat belt.

(b) We should never take out our hands or head out of the window.

(c) We should never disturb the driver.

(d) We should stand on the seat.

48. **The given picture shows a list of safety rules that Kiran's mother prepared for her to follow at home and fixed it on the fridge door. While opening the door of the fridge, Kiran's father accidentally touched the list with wet hands and few words got erased from it. (2021)**

- **Do not touch a you may get a cut.**
- **Do not touch with wet hands, you may get an electric shock.**
- **Never play with a you may get a burn.**

Select the correct sequence of words that got erased from the list.

(a) Scissor, Candle, Fire cracker (b) Blade, Plugs, Teddy bear

(c) Knife, Switches, Matchbox (d) Broken glass, Bicycle, Umbrella

49. **Unscramble the given letters and select the option that correctly identifies the name of the object which one should wear while riding the given object. (2022)**

(a) TALOF (b) TEEMLH

(c) TOINCAAR (d) SKETAS

50. Which combination of statements is correct? (2022)

1. Throwing garbage into a river causes water pollution.

2. Water provides a home to live to a large variety of animals.

3. Rainwater does not help plants to grow.

4. Sea-water is blackish in colour.

(a) Only 1 and 2 (b) Only 1, 2 and 3

(c) Only 2 and 3 (d) Only 1 and 4

RESPONSE GRID

LEVEL 1

1. a b c d	2. a b c d	3. a b c d	4. a b c d	5. a b c d
6. a b c d	7. a b c d	8. a b c d	9. a b c d	10. a b c d
11. a b c d	12. a b c d	13. a b c d	14. a b c d	15. a b c d
16. a b c d	17. a b c d	18. a b c d	19. a b c d	20. a b c d
21. a b c d	22. a b c d	23. a b c d	24. a b c d	25. a b c d
26. a b c d	27. a b c d	28. a b c d	29. a b c d	30. a b c d
31. a b c d	32. a b c d	33. a b c d	34. a b c d	35. a b c d
36. a b c d	37. a b c d	38. a b c d	39. a b c d	40. a b c d
41. a b c d	42. a b c d	43. a b c d		

LEVEL 2

1. a b c d	2. a b c d	3. a b c d	4. a b c d	5. a b c d
6. a b c d	7. a b c d	8. a b c d	9. a b c d	10. a b c d
11. a b c d	12. a b c d	13. a b c d	14. a b c d	15. a b c d
16. a b c d	17. a b c d	18. a b c d	19. a b c d	20. a b c d
21. a b c d	22. a b c d	23. a b c d	24. a b c d	25. a b c d
26. a b c d	27. a b c d	28. a b c d	29. a b c d	30. a b c d
31. a b c d	32. a b c d	33. a b c d	34. a b c d	35. a b c d
36. a b c d	37. a b c d	38. a b c d	39. a b c d	40. a b c d
41. a b c d	42. a b c d	43. a b c d	44. a b c d	45. a b c d
46. a b c d	47. a b c d	48. a b c d	49. a b c d	50. a b c d

Solutions with Explanation

LEVEL- 1

1. (c) We must exercise daily to keep ourself healthy.
2. (c) We use nailcutter to cut our nails.
3. (a) We should sit on a chair with our back straight.
4. (a) We use soap to wash our body.
5. (d) We use tooth brush to clean our teeth.
6. (a) We brush our teeth after waking up in the morning.
7. (b) Washing hands with soap removes dirt and germs from our hands thereby reducing the chances of germs entering into our mouth while eating with hands.
8. (d) We should cover our mouth when we are sneezing, coughing and yawning.
9. (c) You should always walk on the zebra crossing when you are crossing the road.
10. (d) All these are good habits.
11. (a) Figure 'a' is showing good habit that we should always get into a bus in a line.
12. (d) Always use swimming tubes, floaters or arm bands while swimming.
13. (b) The figure in option b shows a child playing with electrical plug socket, which might give him an electric shock.
14. (d) All the activities are not safe.
15. (b) First Aid is the immediate help given to a person who is hurt, before the doctor comes.
16. (a) The given option a denotes safety rules on the road. One must always cross the road at zebra crossing. Option (b), (c) and (d) show unsafe habits. We should not run after a moving bus or on the road. We should not play with wires.
17. (b) We should take bath every morning
18. (c)
19. (a) We should always play in a playground as it is safe to play there.
20. (b)
21. (b) Child in the option 'b' is brushing his teeth. We should brush our teeth every morning and at night before going to bed.

22. (c)

23. (d) In the option 'a', the child is playing with fire. In option 'B', child is trimming the plants using sharp tool by himself. In option 'C', child is running after a moving bus. So, no child is following the safety rule.

24. (a) 25. (c) 26. (b) 27. (b)

28. (d) In the options 'd', child is throwing seeds of watermelon anywhere which is a bad habit.

29. (a) On footpath, always walk on your left side.

30. (c)

31. (d) We should take bath, brush our teeth and take breakfast daily.

32 (d) 33. (b) 34. (c) 35 (a)

36. (a) 37. (a) 38. (c)

39. (b) HMETEL → HELMET, which is worn while cycling.

40. (b)

41. (d) Crossing the road using zebra crossing is a good habit.

42. (d) 43. (d)

LEVEL- 2

1. (a) breakfast
2. (b) meal
3. (b) exercise
4. (a) bones
5. (b) good
6. (a) healthy
7. (b) Without rest we can fall ill, sleep for 8 hours everyday, eat healthy to stay healthy. Exercise help us to keep fit.
8. (b) Never bite your nails, use nail cutter to cut your nails.
9. (c) Playground is the correct place for playing football and running while bathroom is the correct place to take bath.
10. (c) It is a set of painted lines on the road for safe crossing.
11. (d) We keep our hair clean with the help of SHAMPOO, which is hidden in the given word grid.
12. (d) We should give some first aid to him/her before taking him/her to the hospital.
13. (d) The given picture shows that Raman is playing in park. Playing makes muscles stronger, increases stamina of body and keeps its fit. We should play and do physical activities everyday.

14. (b) Wash your hands with soap to clean them off dirt.

15. (c) We must keep our body clean to stay fit and healthy. Riya takes bath twice daily and Swati never throws garbage on road, these are good habits Whereas, Ram who does not brush his teeth at night, has a bad habit.

16. (a) We must take bath and get ready by wearing uniform, then we should comb our hair. After that, we should go to our school.

17. (a) We must take breakfast every morning and brush our teeth and comb our hair daily.

18. (c) It is not necessary to wash hands before going to toilet.

19. (a) Rajat is walking down to his home and he must obey traffic rules. Option 1 and 4 are the correct signals for a pedestrain to safely cross the road at a zebra crossing, whereas, option 2 and 4 are correct signals for vehicles to move on the road.

20. (c)

21. (c) We should not get in or get out of a moving bus.

22. (d) A child can play with teddy bear alone.

23. (d) We should give some first aid to the injured person before taking him to hospital.

24. (a) safety

25. (b) run

26. (b) footpath

27. (a) zebra

28. (d) We should not fly kites on the open terrace because in can be dangerous.

29. (b) Yellow light indicates to stop a while and go.

30. (d) We should NOT play and burn crackers in the middle of the road.

31. (a) We should not touch electric switches with wet hands.

32. (a)

33. (b)	34. (b)	35. (d)	36. (d)
37. (d)	38. (b)	39. (c)	40. (c)
41. (d)	42 (c)	43 (d)	
44. (d)	45. (b)	46 (b)	

47. (d) We should never stand on the seat.

48. (c) You can get a cut from knife. You can get shock if you touch switches from wet hand. Matchbox can cause burns.

49. (b) HELMET

50. (a)

6 CHAPTER FOREWORD

Your family, friends and neighbours play an important role in life.
You all love your family members and friends.

In the blank space given below, paste a photograph of your family and write suitable words to fill the blank.

This is my family...

There are ______________ members in my family.

I have ______________ brothers and ___________ sisters in my family.

We like to ____ together.

After reading of this chapter, you will know about different types of houses, families, friends and neighbourhood. You will also know about different types of occupations.

6 Chapter

Our Home, Family, Friends and Neighbours

Historical Preview

- In ancient times, early man used to live in jungles, eat plants and dead animals, wear the leaves of trees. They did not have any house to live or clothes to wear.

Real Life Examples

(a) Igloo is found in Arctic and greenland's Thule area or polar regions etc.

(b) Huts are found in villages

LEARNING OBJECTIVES

This lesson will help you to:

- Know about the different types of materials used to build house.
- Learn about the different types of houses i.e. kutcha house and pukka house.
- Understand different relationship of the family.
- Study about our school, teachers, neighbours and friends.

INTRODUCTION

We all need a shelter to live as we cannot live on the road. Why do we build house? We build house to protect us from rain, snow, heat, wind and animals.

Different types of materials are used to build houses. For example: People use wood, bricks, stone and mud to make their houses.

On the basis of materials used, houses ore classified into different types.

1. **Kutcha House** : Houses made up of wood and bamboo are known as kutcha house.

   For example : Hut

2. **Pucca House** : Houses made up of bricks, cement etc., are called pucca or pukka house. These are also known as permanent house.

   For example : Flats, Bungalows, Apartments.

   In pucca house, for example in flats and bungalows there are many facilities. There are many rooms for different purposes and activities. Let us study this in detail:

1. **Kitchen** : My mother cooks tasty food for me and my sister in the kitchen.

2. **Drawing Room** : We welcome our guests in the drawing room.

3. **Bedroom** : We take rest and sleep in the bedroom.

4. **Bathroom** : We take bath and wash our clothes in the bathroom.

FAMILY

I live with my mother and father in my sweet home but my best friend Shiva lives with his mother, father, elder sister, grandmother and grandfather. We all live together with love. We are all family.

Let us study more about family in detail.

We all live in a house with our father, mother, brother and sister together as a family. Father and mother together are called **parents**. Family may be big and small.

(Small Family)

Small family : In a small family, there are parents and two or three children. This is also known as a nuclear family.

Big family : In a big family, there are parents, brother, sister, grandfather, grandmother all living together.

- Every member of a family has a very important role and is needed by all other members.
- Members of a family have a common name. This is known as surname. Some members are called by a short name called nick name or pet name.
- In some families not only parents and children but also uncle, aunt, their children along with grand parents live together. Such a family is called joint family.
- Brother of our father is called uncle and his wife is our aunt. Sister of our father is also called aunt.
- Brother of our mother is known as maternal uncle.
- Uncle's children are our cousins.

(Big Family)

(Joint Family)

Neighbourhood : My best friend Shiva lives near to my house. We play together every evening in the park. He also helps me in doing my homework.

Shiva's mother and my mother both are best friends. We are neighbours.

The surrounding area near house is known as neighbourhood.

School : Shiva and I go to school together. He is my classmate. In school we meet our other friends also. School is a place where we study and learn.

1. We learn to read, write and draw.
2. We learn to share our things with others.
3. We learn many games and take part in sports and other activities.

Classmate : Friends of same class in a school are known as classmates.

OCCUPATION

In school, a number of people work.

1. **Teacher** : Teacher teaches us different subjects.

2. **Gardener** : He keeps our garden and playground proper and grows plants, flowers and grasses wherever required.
3. **Sweeper** : He keeps our classroom campus clean and tidy.
4. **Gate keeper** : He takes care of the school gate and keep records of the people visiting our school.
5. **Principal** : Principal is the head of the school.

GAMES WE PLAY

Playing different types of games is very important for the growth and development of every child. We play many games with our friends in school play ground, park as well as at our home.

Games that are played outside the house are called

Outdoor games.

For Example : Badminton, tennis, cricket, footballs, basketball etc.

Outdoor games

Some games can be played inside the house and are known as **indoor games**.

For Example : Carrom, chess, ludo, snake ladder, video games etc.

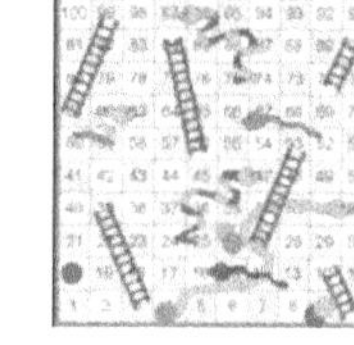

Indoor games

Multiple Choice Questions

LEVEL- 1

1. **Our home protects us from __________.**

   (a) rain (b) wind

   (c) animals (d) All of these

2. **In which of the following rooms, we take rest?** **[2012]**

   (a) Kitchen (b) Bedroom

   (c) Bathroom (d) Drawing room

3. **A family that consists of mother, father and children is known as __________.** **[Tricky]**

   (a) joint family (b) small family (c) big family (d) good family

4. **Ramesh is the brother of my father. He is my ________.** **[Tricky]**

   (a) aunt (b) uncle

   (c) cousin (d) none of the above

5. **Reena and Sheena are my uncle's children. They both are my ________.**

   (a) brother (b) sister (c) cousin (d) aunt

6. **Which of the following place we use to study and learn?** **[2013]**

   (a) Hospital (b) School

   (c) Kitchen (d) Drawing room

7. **This type of family is known as ___________.** **[Tricky]**

   (a) small family (b) joint family

   (c) big family (d) both (b) and (c)

8. Which of the following is an INCORRECT match?

(a) Grandfather's wife - Grandmother

(b) Uncle's wife - Aunt

(c) Mother's father - Grandfather

(d) Uncle's son - Nephew

9. Which of these shows your contribution as a helping hand in your family?

(a) 

(b) 

(c) 

(d) All of these

10. Which of the following is a kutcha house?

(a) Apartment (b) Flat

(c) Hut (d) None of these

11. The surrounding area near our house is known as ________. **[2014]**

(a) school (b) neighbourhood

(c) family (d) temple

12. Our house keeps us safe from ___________.

(a) heat, cold and family (b) rain, winds and food

(c) heat, cold and rain (d) cold, winds and school

13. Which of these is least likely to be found in the kitchen? [2015]

(a) 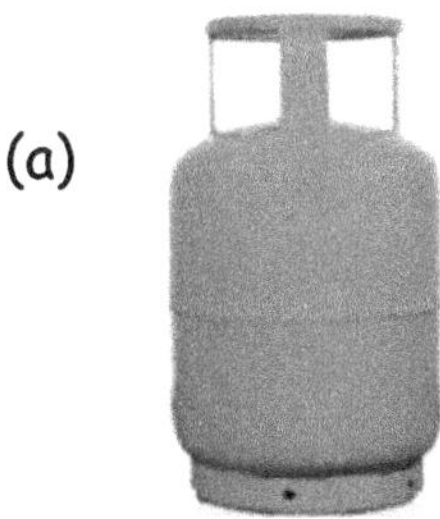

(b) 

(c) 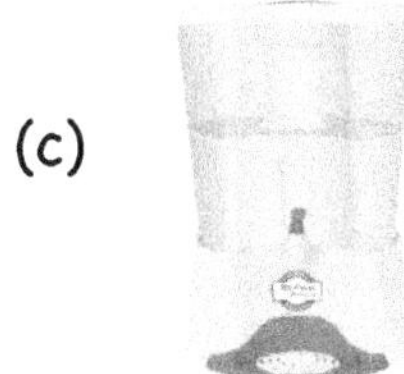

(d) 

14. Pucca house is made up of ________.

(a) snow (b) brick

(c) wood (d) none of these

15. Members of a family have one word common in their names. It is called as _______. [Tricky]

(a) Nick name (b) Pet name (c) First name (d) Surname

16. Ravi lives with his father, mother, grand mother, uncle, aunt and cousin. Ravi is living in a ________ family.

(a) joint family (b) big family

(c) small family (d) both (a) and (b)

17. If myself, the only son, is living with my father and mother in New Delhi, then my family has how many members? [Tricky]

(a) Two (b) Three (c) Four (d) Five

18. ________ is the head of the school.

(a) Principal (b) Teacher

(c) Gatekeeper (d) None of the above

19. The person who teaches us in schools is our _______.

(a) Watchman (b) Sweeper

(c) Teacher (d) None of these

20. People who live near our houses are our _______.

(a) teachers (b) classmates (c) neighbours (d) friends

21. All the members of Rohan's family pray to God before their meal. This is a: [Tricky]

(a) Custom (b) Celebration (c) Compulsion (d) Punishment

22. Just as a family member is an important part of the family, the family is an Important part of:

(a) The house (b) The school (c) The Society (d) None of these

23. Which of the following statements is correct? [Tricky]

(a) All families are similar

(b) The elder members of the family do not require the support of the younger members

(c) All families have only two members

(d) None of the above

24. A doctor who treats animals is called as: [2016]

(a) Gatekeeper (b) Vet (c) Principal (d) None of these

25. Savitri is performing a wrong activity, as shown in the picture. Select the correct option to justify this. [Tricky]

(a) Living room is for meeting guests and not for cooking.

(b) It is extremely dangerous to cook in furniture filled room as things may catch fire from cooking stove.

(c) Living room will get dirty and untidy.

(d) All of these

26. In which of these rooms of our house, we take a nap? [2014]

(a) 

(b) 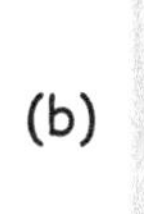 

(c) 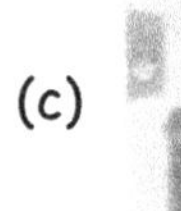 

(d) 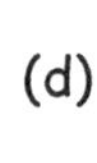 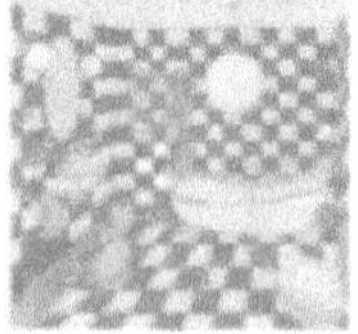

27. Refer to the given conversation between two friends. [2016]

Priya: Hello Nidhi! So nice to see you. Please have a seat.

Nidhi: Thanks Priya. It's been a long time since we met.

In which of the following rooms are Nidhi and Priya most likely present?

(a) 

(b) 

(c) 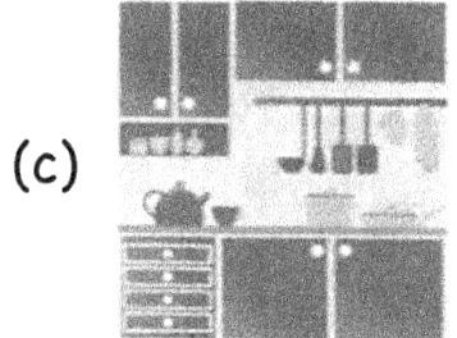

(d) 

28. Rahul is the brother of Gitanjali and father of Mayank. What will Mayank call Gitanjali? [Critical Thinking]

(a) Mother
(b) Sister
(c) Aunt
(d) Sister-in-law

29. Solve the given crossword having names of things used in our home. In which of these rooms of the house, the hidden things are NOT used? [2013]

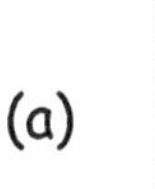

(a) 

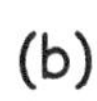

(b) 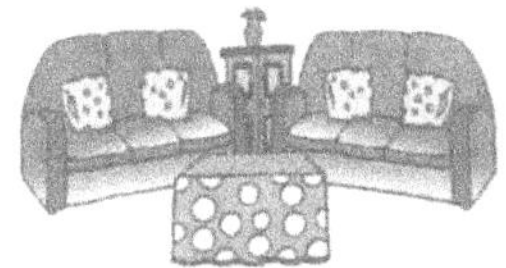

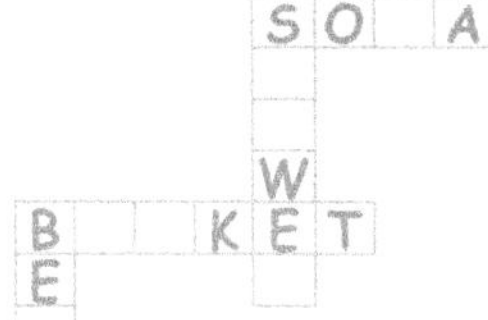

(c) 

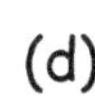

(d) 

30. You are living in a joint family with parents, uncle, aunt, cousin and grandmother. Everyone loves you very much. Which of these work you could do in your family to help your family members?

(a) You can play with them.
(b) You can earn money.
(c) You can set table for meals.
(d) You can paint the doors.

31. In which of these rooms of our house, do we attend our guests?

(a) 

(b) 

(c) 

(d) 

32. Which of the following activity we learn at school? **[Tricky]**

(a) We learn to read and write.

(b) We learn to fight.

(c) We learn to share our things with each other.

(d) Both (a) and (c).

33. The woman in picture 1 is cooking food in wrong room. Now, refer to the picture 2 and select the correct place for cooking. **[2015]**

Picture 1

Picture 2

(a) e (b) g (c) h (d) f

34. If my family consists of 4 members, in that case the fourth member of my family will be my __________. **[Tricky]**

(a) Sister (b) Teacher (c) gardener (d) all of these

35. Identify X, Y and Z. **[2013, Tricky]**

Family	Grandmother	'X'	Uncle
Pucca house	'Y'	Flats	Apartment
Small family	Father	Children	'Z'

(a) X = Teacher, Y = Father, Z = Uncle

(b) X = Aunt, Y = Hut, Z = Teacher

(c) X = Father, Y = Bungalow, Z = Mother

(d) X = Father, Y = Hut, Z = Aunt

36. Solve the given crossword to find the number of homes; [2014]

(a) Built by animals themselves

(b) Built by man for domestic animals

(a) a - 3, b - 1

(b) a - 2, b - 2

(c) a - 3, b - 2

(d) a - 1, b - 3

→ ↓

S	K	H	N
H	I	V	E
E	I	P	S
D	T	Y	T
R	M	W	A
N	W	E	B
Z	S	A	L
C	E	R	E

37. Which of these is least likely to be found in the kitchen? **(2018)**

(a) (b) (c) (d)

38. Which of the following rooms is used for cooking food? (2020)

(a) (b) (c) (d)

39. Deepika's sister's son is her __________ (2020)

(a) Cousm (b) Nephew (c) Niece (d) Brother

40. If Payal's mother has two sisters and one brother, then how many children does Payal's maternal grandfather has? (2021)

(a) Two (b) Three (c) Four (d) One

41. We use different things to keep our house clean. Why do we use a mop? (2022)

(a) For cooking food

(b) For cleaning the utensils

(c) For wiping the floor

(d) All of these

LEVEL 2

Directions (Qs. 1 - 10): Fill in the blanks in the passage given below.

House ________ (1) ________ us from rain, snow, heat and wind. People use wood, brick, and stones to make their ________ (2) ________. Kutcha house is made up of ________(3) ________. My mother cooks tasty food for me in the ________(4) ________. We welcome our ________(5) ________ in the drawing room. Brother of our father is called ________(6) ________. Uncle's children are my ________(7) ________. ________(8) ________ is the place where we study and learn. Friends of same class in a school are known as ________(9). All ________(10) of a family are very important. **[Critical Thinking]**

1. (a) helps (b) protects
(c) damages (d) scares

2. (a) water (b) house
(c) food (d) none of these

3. (a) mud (b) water
(c) bricks (d) none of these

4. (a) kitchen (b) bedroom
(c) drawing room (d) garden

5. (a) brother (b) guest
(c) house (d) none of these

6. (a) uncle (b) aunt
(c) cousins (d) grand father

7. (a) aunt (b) wife
(c) cousins (d) mother

8. (a) School (b) Hospital
(c) House (d) None of these

9. (a) friends (b) classmates
(c) family (d) neighbour

10. (a) fathers (b) members
(c) cousins (d) uncles

11. **Match the Column I with Column II:**

Column I		Column II	
A.	Kutcha House	1.	Father
B.	Pucca House	2.	Mud
C.	School	3.	Bricks
D.	Family	4.	Teachers

	A	B	C	D
(a)	1	3	4	2
(b)	2	3	4	1
(c)	1	3	2	4
(d)	1	2	3	4

12. **Who among the following is NOT a family member?** **[2014]**

(a) Uncle (b) Wife (c) Grandfather (d) Teacher

13. **Rama is married to Satish. Rama is _______ of Satish?**

(a) Aunt (b) Wife (c) Grandmother (d) Teacher

14. **The brother of your mother will be your ______.**

(a) aunt (b) grandmother

(c) maternal uncle (d) none of these

Directions (Qs. 15 to 19): Read the following paragraph and answer the following questions. **[Critical Thinking]**

We go to school every morning with our friends. There we see a man who cleans the school and classroom daily and a person who keeps our garden clean and grows plants and flowers in the garden. In school our teacher teaches us good habits. We learn many things in the school as well as we play games with our friends in the school playground. For example cricket, volley ball, basket ball etc.

15. **Which of the following is an outdoor game?**

(a) Chess (b) Cricket

(c) Volley ball (d) Both (b) & (c)

16. **Who teaches us good habits?**

(a) Watchman (b) Gardener

(c) Teacher (d) None of these

17. **Who cleans our school and classroom daily?**

(a) Gardener (b) Sweeper (c) Teacher (d) Friend

18. **We go to _______ every morning.**

(a) school (b) playground

(c) church (d) none of these

19. **Who grows flowers in the school garden?** **[2015]**

(a) Teacher (b) Gardener (c) Sweeper (d) Friends

20. **Father and mother together are called _______.** **[2014]**

(a) family (b) aunt

(c) parents (d) none of these

21. Count the total number of family members from the given box.

Father	Uncle	Gardener	Cousin
Teacher	Principal	Gatekeeper	Grandmother

(a) 5 (b) 6 (c) 7 (d) 4

22. Vasudhi is the mother of Brijesh. Brijesh is the father of Meera. What will Meera call Vasudhi? [2016, Tricky]

(a) Aunt (b) Mother

(c) Grand mother (d) Niece

23. Rajiv is the brother of Niti and father of Tina. What will Tina call Niti? [2017, Tricky]

(a) Sister (b) Mother (c) sister-in-law (d) Aunt

Directions (Qs. 24 - 26): Find the odd one out.

24. (a) Mud (b) Straw (c) Brick (d) Bamboo

[Tricky]

25. (a) Flat (b) Bungalow (c) Apartment (d) Hut

26. (a) Principal (b) Teacher (c) Gatekeeper (d) Mother

27. Encircle the odd thing from the following **(2019)**

(a) Table (b) Sofa set (c) Bucket (d) chair

28. Refer to the given family tree of Tanvi's family and select the correct statement regarding it. (2021)

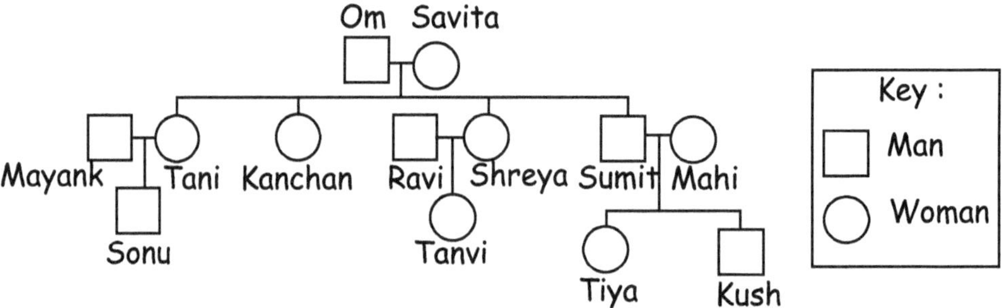

(a) Tanvi is Savita's daughter.

(b) Tiya is Mayank's sibling.

(c) Sonu is Kanchan's nephew.

(d) Om and Savita have four grandsons.

RESPONSE GRID

LEVEL 1

1. a b c d	2. a b c d	3. a b c d	4. a b c d	5. a b c d
6. a b c d	7. a b c d	8. a b c d	9. a b c d	10. a b c d
11. a b c d	12. a b c d	13. a b c d	14. a b c d	15. a b c d
16. a b c d	17. a b c d	18. a b c d	19. a b c d	20. a b c d
21. a b c d	22. a b c d	23. a b c d	24. a b c d	25. a b c d
26. a b c d	27. a b c d	28. a b c d	29. a b c d	30. a b c d
31. a b c d	32. a b c d	33. a b c d	34. a b c d	35. a b c d
36. a b c d	37. a b c d	38. a b c d	39. a b c d	40. a b c d
41. a b c d				

LEVEL 2

1. a b c d	2. a b c d	3. a b c d	4. a b c d	5. a b c d
6. a b c d	7. a b c d	8. a b c d	9. a b c d	10. a b c d
11. a b c d	12. a b c d	13. a b c d	14. a b c d	15. a b c d
16. a b c d	17. a b c d	18. a b c d	19. a b c d	20. a b c d
21. a b c d	22. a b c d	23. a b c d	24. a b c d	25. a b c d
26. a b c d	27. a b c d	28. a b c d		

Solutions with Explanation

LEVEL- 1

1. **(d)** Our home protects us from rain, wind and animals.
2. **(b)** We take rest in bedroom.
3. **(b)** A Small family consists of mother, father and children.
4. **(b)** Brother of my father is my uncle.
5. **(c)** Uncle's children are my cousins.
6. **(b)** School is the place where we use to study and learn.
7. **(d)** This is both a joint family and big family.
8. **(d)** Uncle's son is known as cousin.
9. **(d)**

10. (c) Hut is a kutcha house.

11. (b) Neighbourhood is the surrounding area near our house.

12. (c) House keeps us safe from heat, cold and rain.

13. (b) Sofa is not found in kitchen. It is found in drawing room.

14. (b) Pucca house is made up of bricks.

15. (d) Surname is the word that is common in the names of the members of a family.

16. (a) Ravi is living in a joint family.

17. (b) There will be three members in my family.

18. (a) Principal is the head of school.

19. (c) Teacher teaches us in school.

20. (c) Neighbours live near our house.

21. (a) 22. (a) 23. (d) 24. (b)

25. (d) 26. (b)

27. (a) We greet our guests in living or drawing room (option a). Hence Nidhi and Priya are most likely present in drawing room. Option (b) is bedroom, (c) is kitchen and (d) is bathroom.

28. (c) Geetanjali is the sister of Mayank's father so Mayank will call her aunt.

29. (d) The names of the things hidden in the crossword are SOFA, SHOWER, BUCKET and BED. We do not use these things in the dining room. BED is used in the bedroom, SOFA is used in the living room and BUCKET and SHOWER are used in the bathroom.

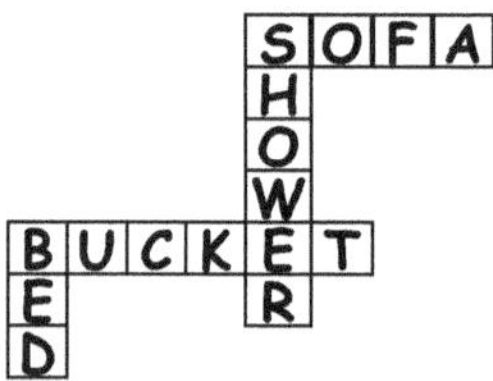

30. (c) You can help your family members by setting table for meals.

31. (c) In drawing room we use to welcome our guests.

32. (d) We learn to read, write and share our things with each other in school.

33. **(c)** In the given picture 2, 'd' and 'f' show bedroom to take rest and sleep, 'e' is a washroom to take bath, 'g' is a living room where we sit with our guests and 'h' is a kitchen to cook food. The given picture 1 shows living room and is not used for cooking food. 'h' in the picture 2 is kitchen and is the correct place to cook food.

34. **(a)** Sister will be the fourth member of the family.

35. **(c)** X is father who is a family member.

Y is bungalow which is a pucca house.

Z is mother who is a member of a small family.

36. **(c)**

37. **(b)**

38. **(c)**

39. **(b)**

40. **(c)** Payal's grand father has children = Payal's mother + Two sisters + One brother = 4

41. **(c)** For wiping floor.

LEVEL- 2

1. **(b)** protects

2. **(b)** house

3. **(a)** mud

4. **(a)** kitchen

5. **(b)** guests

6. **(a)** uncle

7. **(c)** cousins

8. **(a)** school

9. **(b)** classmates

10. **(b)** members

11. (b) Kutcha house is made up of mud, pucca house is made up of bricks, teacher teaches in school, father is member of family.

12. (d) Teacher is NOT a family member.

13. (b) Rama is the wife of Satish.

14. (c) Brother of your mother is your maternal uncle.

15. (d) Cricket and volleyball are outdoor games.

16. (c) Teacher teaches us good habits.

17. (b) Sweeper cleans our classroom daily.

18. (a) We go to school every morning.

19. (b) Gardener grows flowers in the school garden.

20. (c) Father and mother together are called parents.

21. (d) Total number of family members in the box are 4. (Father, Uncle, Cousin, Grandmother)

22. (c) Grand Mother

23. (d) Aunt

24. (c) Brick is used to build pucca house. Mud, straw and bamboo is used to make kutcha house.

25. (d) Hut is a kutcha house. Flat, bungalow and apartment are pucca house.

26.. (d) Mother is a family member.

27. (c) Bucket is the odd thing from the given option. Table, sofa set and chair all are found in the drawing room.

28. (c) Kanchan is the sister of Sonu's mother Tani. Therfore, Sonu is the nephew of Kanchan.

7 CHAPTER FOREWORD

We all need air and water to live. Air is all around us. We cannot see air but can feel it. Water is needed by all the plants and animals. We get water from rivers, lakes, ponds, wells etc.

Here is an interesting activity that you can do. This activity will make you feel the presence of air around you.

EXPERIENCE THE WIND

Things you will need:

- A brown paper bag
- Ribbon, streamers and yarn
- Markers
- Stapler or tape

METHOD:

- Cut the bottom of the paper bag.
- At the top of the bag, punch 2 holes across each other. Cut the yarn to use as a handle and string it through the two holes and tie the ends together.
- Decorate the bag with markers.
- Staple or tape streamers around the bottom of the bag.
- Run outside with it to experience the wind or hang it outside to watch the wind.

After reading this chapter, you will understand the importance of air and water. You will also know about different seasons.

7

Chapter

Air, Water and Weather

Amazing Fact

❖ On Earth, we are lucky to have an atmosphere filled with air. The air in our atmosphere acts as insulation, keeping the Earth from getting too cold or too hot.

LEARNING OBJECTIVES

This lesson will help you to:

❖ Study about the importance of air and water.

❖ Learn about different types of seasons.

❖ Know about sun, moon and stars.

INTRODUCTION

Have you filled air in your bicycle or in footballs. Air gives shape to objects. Let us know more about Air.

AIR: Air is present all around us. We can feel the air when it moves but we can't see air. All living things need air to breathe. Without air, there will be no life on the earth.

Uses of Air:

- Plants and animals need air to breathe.
- Balloon and football are filled with air.
- Air has weight.
- Fire needs air to burn

Air cannot be seen, we can only feel air. Moving air is called wind. The slow moving wind is called **breeze**. The fast moving wind is called **storm** which can damage your house.

Real Life Examples

(a) Air is used to dry clothes

(b) Air is used to fill tyres, football, balloon etc.

WATER:

Water is needed for life. Plants and animals need water. Water is present in oceans, river, lakes, ponds etc. We need water for drinking, bathing, cooking and washing etc.

Do You Know?

- Water covers around 70% of the earth's surface.

Drinking Bathing

Cooking Washing

WATER CONSERVATION

Water is very essential for our life. Life is not possible without water. Water can be stored in dams, wells, ponds, rivers, lakes etc. We should not waste water. Water can be reused for various purposes such as cleaning, washing, irrigation etc. This is called water conservation.

WEATHER:

Weather is the condition of the environment during a short or a long period of time. We have mainly the following types of weather:

1) **Summer:** In summers, days are very hot. We wear cotton clothes in summer.

2) **Autumn:** In this weather, trees shed their leaves. The weather is neither too hot nor too cold.

Misconcept/Concept

- **Misconcept:** Stars are very very small in size.

  Concept: Stars are large in size, they appear small because they are far away from us.
- **Misconcept:** Moon has its own light

  Concept: Moon does not have its own light. Moon shines because the light of sun falls on it

Do You Know?

- Rakesh Sharma was the first Indian to go to space in 1984.

Amazing Fact

- Sun which gives us bright light in the day, is actually a star. Sun is the closest star that is why it appears big as compared to other stars.

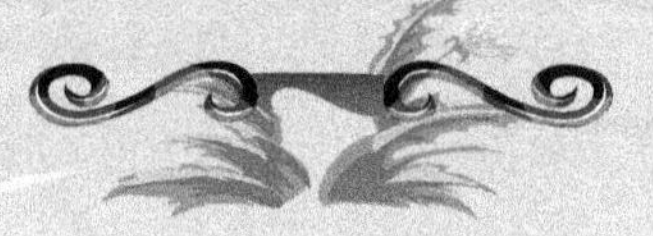

3) **Spring:** In this weather, new leaves grow on trees and different flowers bloom.

4) **Winter:** In this weather, days and night are very cold. We wear woollen clothes in winter.

5) **Monsoon:** In this weather, it rains heavily. We need raincoat and umbrella in this weather.

Weather depends upon Sun, clouds and wind.

1. Sun: Sun rises in the east and sets in the west. The Sun is round and very hot. It is very big. It gives us light and heat. Sun is also a star.

2. Moon: The Moon shines at night. The Moon looks like a big white ball. The shape of the Moon changes every night. When the moon is big & round, it is called full moon. Moon does not have its own light.

3. Star: We see stars in the sky at night. Stars are very far from us, that is why they appear very small. They have their own light.

Multiple Choice Questions

LEVEL 1

1. **In which of these seasons, weather is neither hot nor cold?**
   (a) Spring (b) Autumn (c) Winter (d) Both (a) & (b)
2. **The Sun gives us __________.**
   (a) night (b) heat and light (c) water (d) air
3. **and are filled with __________.** **[2015]**
   (a) water (b) air (c) sand (d) fire
4. **For lighting we need __________.**
   (a) water (b) food (c) air (d) all of these
5. **Look at the picture given below. It is due to __________.**
   (a) breeze (b) storm (c) pollution (d) waves
6. **Cotton clothes are preferred during _________ season.** **[2012]**
   (a) rainy (b) summer (c) winter (d) spring
7. **We wear raincoat in ____________.**
   (a) rainy season (b) winter season
   (c) summer season (d) All of these
8. **The very strong wind with rain or snow is called ________________.** **[Tricky]**
   (a) Gale (b) Storm (c) Breeze (d) Dew

9. The picture shows a rainy day. **[2013, Tricky]**

What do you use on a rainy day?

(a) Woollen sweater (b) Cotton shirt

(c) Raincoat and umbrella (d) Woollen cap and gloves

10. What is the moon called when it is big and round? **[Tricky]**

(a) No moon (b) New moon (c) Full moon (d) Half moon

11. The sun rises in the ________.

(a) east (b) west (c) north (d) south

12. Which of the following is INCORRECT? **[Tricky]**

1. Weather changes from day to day.

2. Weather changes only once during the day.

3. Days may be sunny, windy, rainy or cloudy.

(a) 3 only (b) 1 and 2 (c) 2 only (d) 2 and 3

13. Water covers around __________ of the earth's surface.

(a) 70% (b) 65% (c) 35% (d) 20%

14. Select an INCORRECT pair. **[Tricky]**

(a) Hot day - Gumboots (b) Rainy day - Umbrella

(c) Cold day - Bonfire (d) Sunny day - Sunglasses

15. On which of the following factors, weather is NOT dependent? **[Tricky]**

(a) Sun (b) Water (c) Cloud (d) Wind

16. Trees shed their leaves in which of the following season?

(a) Summer (b) Winter (c) Spring (d) Autumn

17. In which of the following season, rainbow is seen?

(a) Summer (b) Spring (c) Monsoon (d) Winters

18. Richa did an activity as shown below. **[Critical Thinking]**

She took an empty glass

She tilted the glass and slowly pushed it down into a tub of water

She observed bubbles coming out of the glass. What does this activity show?

(a) The empty glass is filled with air
(b) Water displaces air in the glass
(c) Air comes out of the water in the form of bubbles
(d) All of these

19. At home, we can store water in _____. **[2015]**

(a) Well, Tank, Hand-pump (b) Well, Hand-pump, Bottles
(c) Buckets, Tank, Bottles (d) Hand-pump, Bottles, Buckets

20. In which of these seasons, weather is neither hot nor cold? **[2015]**

(a) Spring (b) Summer (c) Winter (d) Both a and b

21. Which of these words does NOT rhyme with any water body present on Earth? **[Tricky]**

Clue – Bond : Pond

(a) Shiver (b) Cake (c) Bug (d) Bring

22. The given figure shows that moving air **[Critical Thinking]**

(a) Has no weight (b) Has direction
(c) Can be seen (d) Cannot dry clothes

23. Which of the following is NOT a shape of Moon ? **[2015]**

(a) Full Moon (b) Half Moon (c) New Moon (d) Old Moon

24. One of the three things which makes the air dirty is given in the word grid. Find the names of the other two things and match them with the pictures of their respective sources. **[Critical Thinking]**

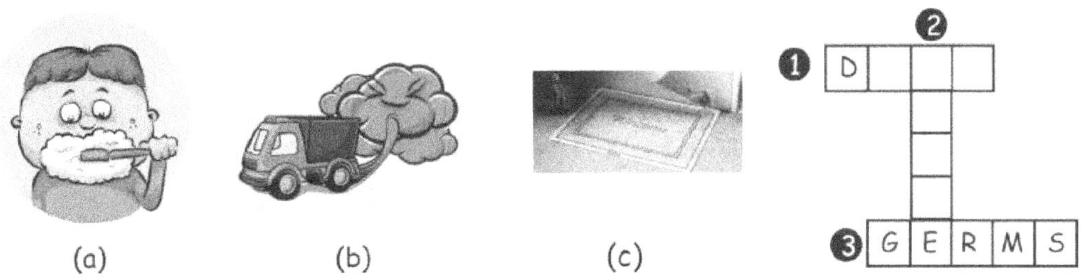

(a) 1-(b), 2-(a), 3-(c) (b) 1-(c), 2-(a), 3-(b)
(c) 1-(a), 2-(b), 3-(c) (d) 1-(c), 2-(b), 3-(a)

25. I am needed for burning. I am present all around you. You call me as _____. [2015]

(a) Water (b) Soil (c) Sky (d) Air

26. Select the INCORRECT match. [2015]

(a) Sun - Gives light and warmth
(b) Moon - Seems to twinkle in the sky
(c) Stars - Have no light of their own
(d) Both b and c

27. Savitri is mopping the floor. Which of the following would help her in better and faster cleaning? [Tricky]

(a) Dry mop and still air

(b) Wet mop and still air

(c) Dry mop and moving air

(d) Wet mop and moving air

28. On a Full Moon's night, moon looks round like a _____. [2015]

(a) (b) (c) (d)

29. All living things breath air except __________ . [2016]

(a) Fish because they live in water
(b) Plants because they do not move
(c) Earthworms because they live underground
(d) None of these

30. The Sun looks like a big, yellow __________ of fire. [2016]

(a) (b) (c) (d)

31. Phases of Moon are the __________ . [2016]

(a) Spots present of Moon
(b) Stars present aroung Moon
(c) Changing shapes of Moon
(d) Changing of colours of Moon

32. The given table shows the different conditions provided to baby plants A, B, C and D. Which of these plants will remain alive after a week? [2016]

	Air	Sunlight	Water	Soil
(a)	✓	✓	✓	✓
(b)	×	✓	✓	×
(c)	✓	×	×	✓
(d)	✓	✓	×	×

33. Which of these is the shape of the crescent Moon? **[2013]**

(a) (b)  (c) 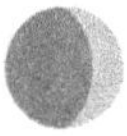 (d) Both a and c

34. For which of these actions, we do not need water ? **[2013]**

(a)  (b)  (c)  (d)

35. Which of these will pollute air around us ? **[2013]**

(a) Using CNG buses (b) Burning of crackers

(c) Throwing factory waste in river (d) Cutting of trees

36. Air moves in a particular direction. This helps us to __________ . **[2013]**

a. Breathe b. Dry clothes c. Sail boats d. Fly kites

(a) a and c (b) b and c (c) c and d (d) b and d

37. What is WRONG about the activity shown in the given picture? **[2014]**

(a) Water is being used from the tap.

(b) Children are playing in the open.

(c) Water is being wasted.

(d) All of the above

38. Which of these activities does NOT need air? **[2014]**

(a)  (b)  (c)  (d)

39. I am present all around you. I am needed for burning. I also help in _________. **(2019)**

(a) Playing flute (b) Breathing (c) Flying kites (d) All of these

40. Which of the following statements about the Moon is corect? **(2020)**

(a) The Moon does not have its own light.

(b) The Moon has air and water on it.

(c) The Moon reflects Earth's light.

(d) Rotation of the Moon gives rise to day and night on Earth.

41. Unscramble the following to find out the name of a deep hole dug to get underground water. (2020)

(a) ATKN (b) UKTCBE (c) MAD (d) ELWL

42. Which of the following activities can be done with the help of air? (2020)

(a) Blowing up a balloon (b) Washing dishes
(c) Washing clothes (d) Mopping the floor

43. The weather forecast of a day during a particular season is shown in the given picture. We should wear ________ on this day. (2020)

(a) Silk saree
(b) Sweater
(c) Cotton frock
(d) Shorts

44. Which among the following has more air? (2020)

(a)  (b) 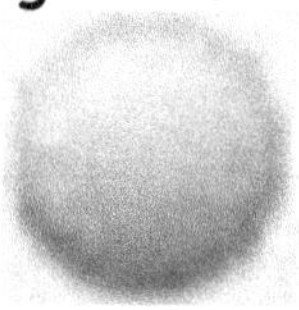 (c) (d)

45. Select the correct statement. (2020)

(a) The Sun shines brightly on rainy days.
(b) It gets hot when the snow falls.
(c) It is very cold in the spring season.
(d) The trees shed their leaves in autumn.

46. Ritvik was drinking hot chocolate on a winter morning. He observed X' over 1he cup. what is 'X? (2020)

(a) Smoke (b) water droplets
(d) water vapour (d) ice crystals

47. Aarav made a list of ways to save water as given here. (2020)

1. Take bath from shower rather than from bucket or tub.
2. Turn off the tap while brushing your teeth.
3. Use a bucket of water and sponge to clean the car.
4. Prefer washing fruits and vegetables in running water instead of a bowl of water.
5. Use watering can to water the plants.

Which of these ways is/are INCORRECT?

(a) 3 only (b) 2, 4 and 5 only (c) I and 5 only (d) 1 and 4 only

48. I am the brightest object in the sky during daytime. I give heat and light. I make life possible on Earth. Who am I? **(2021)**

(a)  (b)  (c)  (d)

49. Which of the following activities does NOT require air? **(2021)**

(a) Burning of gas stove
(b) Drying of clothes
(c) Washing of clothes
(d) Flying of kite

50. Which of the following shows water getting dirty? **(2021)**

(a)  (b)

(c)  (d)

51. The given picture shows ______. **(2021)**

(a) Gibbous Moon (b) Crescent Moon (c) Full Moon (d) New Moon

52. ______ is an underground source of water. **(2022)**

(a) River (b) Pond (c) Well (d) Dam

53. Air is NOT needed for ______.

(a) Cleaning utensils (b) Washing clothes (c) Burning of wood (d) Both a and b

54. A tyre without air becomes flat. This shows that _______.

(a) Air occupies space
(b) Air helps to move things
(c) Air is needed for burning
(d) Air makes things heavy

55. Different patterns made up of stars in the night sky are known as ______. **(2022)**

(a) Planets (b) Clouds (c) Constellations (d) Rainbows

56. Why does size of a balloon increase when air is pumped into it? **(2022)**

(a) Because air occupies space
(b) Because air is invisible to us
(c) Because air has no mass
(d) None of these

57. Which of the following is not the source of fresh water? (2022)

(a) River (b) Ocean (c) Pond (d) Rain

58. Burning garbage to get rid of wastes is: (2022)

(a) a healthy practice and more people should follow it.

(b) an unhealthy practice as it causes air pollution.

(c) good for the environment.

(d) None of these

LEVEL 2

1. Among which of these days you would most likely see rainbow in the sky?

(a) 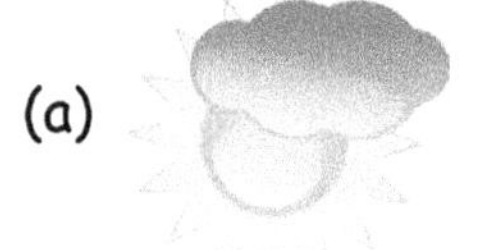 (b)   (c)  (d) 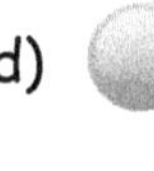 

2. Which of the following statement is correct regarding the moon? [Tricky]

(a) It moves around the sun.

(b) It gives us light at night.

(c) Rakesh Sharma is the first Indian to step on it.

(d) Both (b) and (c)

3. In the given weather chart, which day is sunny and windy? [Tricky]

Day	Monday	Tuesday	Wednesday	Thursday
Morning				
Evening				

(a) Monday (b) Tuesday (c) Wednesday (d) Thursday

4. Match the columns and select the correct option. [Tricky]

Column I		Column II	
A.	Sun	1.	Shines at night
B.	Moon	2.	Twinkle in the sky
C.	Stars	3.	Gives light and heat

	A	B	C		A	B	C
(a)	2	1	3	(b)	3	1	2
(c)	1	2	3	(d)	3	2	1

5. Sonu's grandmother told him that tonight, he can see a Full Moon. What will be the shape of the Moon tonight ? [2015]

(a) 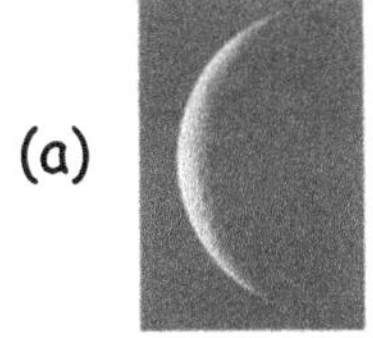 (b) 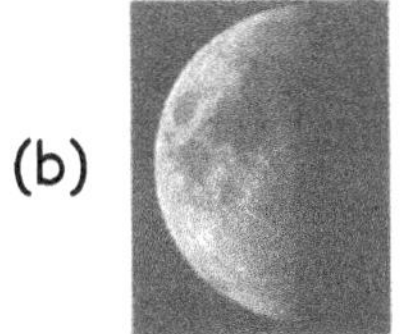 (c) 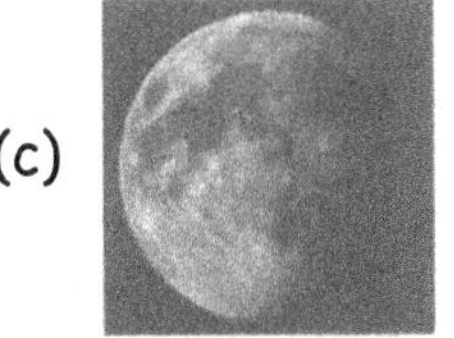 (d) 

6. Select the option by which we get water, present under the ground. [2015]

(a)  (b) 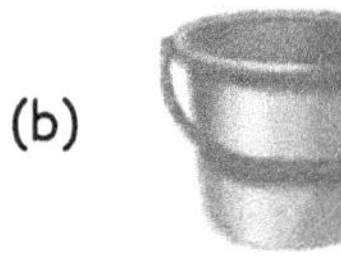 (c)  (d) 

7. Study the given flowchart and identify seasons A, B, C and D

[Critical Thinking]

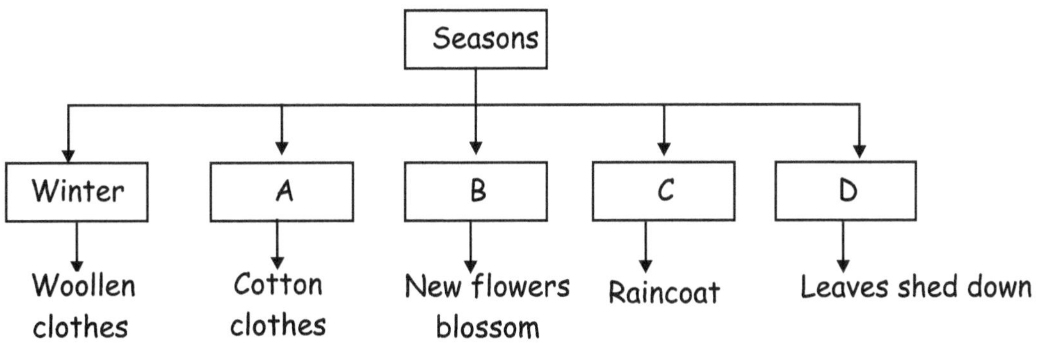

(a) A - Summer, B - Rainy, C - Monsoon, D - Autumn
(b) A - Spring, B - Monsoon, C - Rainy, D - Summer
(c) A - Summer, B - Spring, C - Monsoon, D - Autumn
(d) A - Summer, B - Autumn, C - Rainy, D - Monsoon

8. Tanvi is returning home from school. Which of the following objects she can see in the sky ? [2015]

(a) 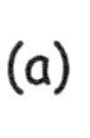  (b)  (c)  (d) All of these

9. **Which of the following is a correct statement ? [2015]**
   (a) Stars look tiny because they appear to change their shape.
   (b) On some nights, the Moon disappears completely. It is called Full Moon.
   (c) All plants and animals depend on the Sun to live.
   (d) Sun is the biggest star in the universe.

10. **Select the option that correctly states the activities done with the help of air and water. [2016]**

	Air	Water
(a)	Swimming	Drying clothes
(b)	Putting out fire	Bathing
(c)	Transportation	Transportation
(d)	Mopping	Cleaning clothes

Direction (Qs. 11 to 20): Fill in the blanks of the passage given below.

[Critical Thinking]

Air is present all around us. We ___(11)___ air when it moves. ___(12)___ air is called Wind. The slow moving air is called ___(13)___ . ___(14)___ can damage your house. We need water for ___(15)___ . There are ___(16)___ seasons. In ___(17)___ , days are very hot. We need ___(18)___ in the monsoon season. The ___(19)___ shines every night and the ___(20)___ of moon changes every night.

11.	(a) see	(b) feel	(c) touch	(d) None of these
12.	(a) Standing	(b) Walking	(c) Moving	(d) Running
13.	(a) breeze	(b) storm	(c) wind	(d) air
14.	(a) Breeze	(b) Storm	(c) Wind	(d) Weather
15.	(a) eating	(b) standing	(c) drinking	(d) both (a) & (c)
16.	(a) three	(b) five	(c) two	(d) six
17.	(a) winter	(b) monsoon	(c) summer	(d) spring
18.	(a) raincoat	(b) icecream	(c) socks	(d) cap
19.	(a) sun	(b) sky	(c) moon	(d) All of these
20.	(a) weight	(b) shape	(c) size	(d) length

21. **Neha was experimenting with two rats. She placed first rat in a box with all the essential things required for living except X. It died within minutes. Then she placed second rat in a box with all things essential for its living except Y. It lived for seven days. What are X and Y respectively? [2016]**

	X	Y
(a)	Food	Water
(b)	Water	Food
(c)	Water	Air
(d)	Air	Food

22. **Read the following statements made by two friends.** **[2016]**

> **Madhu – I can see a bright orange Sun which is looking quite big.**
> **Ram – I can see that Sun is moving down.**

Now select the correct option regarding this.

(a) Only Ram is incorrect because Sun always moves up.

(b) Both Madhu and Ram are correct as they are talking about sunrise.

(c) Both Madhu and Ram are correct as they are talking about sunset.

(d) Only Madhu is incorrect because Sun always appears yellow not orange.

23. **Read the given situation and answer the following questions:** **[2013]**

a. What could he had faced on his way back home?

b. What could he do now?

Nishant has just reached home. His eyes are red and his hair is dirty and dry.

	a	b
(a)	Rain	Take sleep
(b)	Storm	Take bath
(c)	Snow	Take hot drink
(d)	Breeze	Take food

24. **Four students Reema, Latika, Rohan and Amit are discussing about Sun.** **[2014]**

Select the most correct option regarding the statements made by them.

(a) Both Rohan and Latika are correct.

(b) Only Rohan is correct.

(c) Reema is correct and Amit is incorrect.

(d) Only Amit is correct.

25. **A football is filled with air. What changes will it make to the weight of the football?** **[Tricky]**

(a) Its weight will decrease (b) Its weight will increase

(c) No change will occur (d) None of these

26. **Read the following statements and choose the correct answer.** **[Critical Thinking]**

A. The star gives us light in the night.

B. The sun gives us light in the day.

C. The sun changes it shape everyday.

D. The moon changes it shape.

(a) Statements A, B, C are true, D is false.
(b) Statement A, B are true, C and D are false.
(c) Statement A is true, B, C and D are false.
(d) Statements A and C are false, B and D are true.

27. We do not get fresh water from ________

(a) Sea (b) Pond (c) River (d) Rain

28. How can we contribute to keep the air aroung us clean? [2014]

(a) By throwing away garbage in the open
(b) By taking a public bus instead of driving a car
(c) By riding a motorbike to nearby store instead of walking
(d) All of the above

29. The given trees show different weather conditions. Select those weather conditions from the following: [2014]

1 2 3

a. Days are very hot.
b. Days are neither very hot nor very cold.
c. Days are very cold.

(a) 1-a, 2-c, 3-b (b) 1-c, 2-b 3-a
(c) 1-b, 2-a, 3-c (d) 1-c, 2-a, 3-b

30. Which of the following is filled with air?

(a) Football (b) Balloon (c) Tyre (d) All of these

31. In winters, days are very ______.

(a) cold (b) neither hot nor cold
(c) hot (d) rainy

32. Which of these activities can save water?

(a) We should turn off the taps after using.
(b) We should not let the tap run when we brush our teeth.
(c) We should not waste water while bathing.
(d) All of these.

33. Match the columns and select the correct option. [Tricky]

Column - I		Column - II	
A.	Summer days are	1.	Cold
B.	Winter days are	2.	A windy day
C.	A strong wind blows on	3.	Rainy
D.	Monsoon days are	4.	Hot

	A	B	C	D		A	B	C	D
(a)	1	2	3	4	(b)	4	1	2	3
(c)	4	2	1	3	(d)	1	4	3	2

34. Which of the following we use to see in the sky at night?

(a) (b) (c) (d) Both (b) and (c)

35. Which of the following statements is INCORRECT?
(a) Never wash clothes by the river side
(b) Never throw garbage into the river
(c) Drinking pure water can make us sick
(d) We should use water purifier

36. Match the columns and select the correct option. **[Tricky]**

Column-I	Column-II
(A) Drinking impure water	1. Makes the air dirty
(B) While brushing teeth	2. Makes the water dirty
(C) Smoke from the vehicles	3. Turn off the tap
(D) Washing clothes by the river side	4. Can make us sick

(a) A-4, B-3, C-1, D-2 (b) A-2, B-1, C-4, D-3
(c) A-1, B-2, C-3, D-4 (d) A-4, B-3, C-2, D-1

37. Which of the following is Incorrect? **[Tricky]**
(a) Moon does not have its own light (b) Stars are large in size
(c) Stars are very small in size (d) Sun rises in the east

38. Match the columns and select the correct option. **[Tricky]**

Column-I	Column-II
(A) Air	1. Moving air
(B) Wind	2. Air takes up space
(C) Blown up balloon	3. Fast and strong wind
(D) Storm	4. All around us

(a) A-3, B-1, C-4, D-2 (b) A-4, B-1, C-2, D-3
(c) A-4, B-3, C-1, D-2 (d) A-2, B-3, C-4, D-1

39. Which of the following statements is correct? **[Tricky]**
(a) Burning firecrackers makes the air around us dirty
(b) We should burn garbage for fun
(c) Smoke coming out from the vehicles is good for the air
(d) We should drink impure water

Direction (Qs. 40 to 43): Read the following poem carefully and answer the following questions. **[Critical Thinking]**

Air is a gas,
We can't see it that is true
But often we feel it,
In things that we do,
It keeps up a kite
Air fills up a balloon
Without it to breathe
We would be in big trouble

40. Air and _______ plays an important role in life.

(a) animal (b) milk (c) water (d) sun

41. Which of the following object is filled with air?

(a) Car (b) Kite (c) Truck (d) Balloon

42. __________ is the mixture of many gases.

(a) Water (b) Milk (c) Air (d) Animal

43. Living things need air to ________.

(a) eat (b) Drink (c) breathe (d) football

44. Water can be saved by __________. **[Tricky]**

(a)  (b)  (c)  (d)

45. Which of the following is a use of water?

(a) People go to water parks to relax and enjoy
(b) Water is used for putting out fire
(c) We need water to drink
(d) All of these

46. Starting from D, cross (X) out every second letter. Which word will you get? **[Tricky]**

D W T I L N K D

(a) WINK (b) WIND (c) TINK (d) DILK

47. Which of the following statement is INCORRECT?

(a) For lighting a fire, we need air
(b) Rainbow is visible in rainy seasen.
(c) Air is the mixture of only two gases
(d) None of these

48. Complete the following paragraph by choosing the correct sequence of words. **[Tricky]**

We all need __________ to live. Clean water should not be __________. Plants need water to __________. Loss of water can cause a plant to __________.

(a) Air, Thrown, Wilt, Die
(b) Air, Drunk, Grow, Wilt
(c) Water, Wasted, Grow, Wilt
(d) Water, Wasted, Wilt, Die

49. Which of the flowing diagrams shows the shadow of given stick X in the morning? **(2018)**

N
W E
S
X

(a) (b) (c) (d)

50. Which of the following is NOT hidden in the given word grid? **(2018)**

T	B	O	F	W	S	S
D	U	S	T	I	T	E
A	B	Q	A	N	Z	E
P	O	N	D	D	E	X

(a) It is a source of water
(b) It pollutes air.
(c) It is moving air.
(d) It is inflated by air.

51. All lives in Delhi. According to the given weather forecast, which of these should be worn on 4th and 5th July 20XX, respectively? **(2018)**

4th July 20XX 5th July 20XX

	4th July 20XX	**5th July 20XX**
(a)	Raincoat	Woollen sweater
(b)	Gumboots	Woollen gloves
(c)	Woollen sweater	Cotton shirt
(d)	Cotton shirt	Raincoat

52. Payal is looking at the sky and observes that bright and yellow Sun is graduate turning orange. What time of the day does it most likely indicate? **(2019)**

(a) 6 : 00 in the morning
(b) 6 : 00 in the evening
(c) 12 : 00 in the afternoon
(d) 10 : 00 in the morning

53. Match the columns and select the correct option. (2019)

Column I	Column II
(A) Air	1. Moving air
(B) Wind	2. Air takes up space
(C) Blown up balloon	3. Fast and strong wind
(D) Storm	4. All around us

(a) (A)-3, (B)-1, (C)-4, (D)-2
(b) (A)-4, (B)-1, (C)-2, (D)-3
(c) (A)-4, (B)-3, (C)-1, (D)-2
(d) (A)-2, (B)-3, (C)-4, (D)-1

54. Unscramble the given letters and then select the word that is NOT a form of air. (2019)

(a) DINW
(b) EEERZB
(c) NDAS
(d) MOTRS

55. Which of these needs both water and air? (2019)

(a) A moving sail boat
(b) Seed growing into a plant
(c) Drying of wet floor
(d) Both A and B

56. Match column I with column II and select the correct option. (2020)

Column I	**Column II**
A. I give you heat and light.	1. Earth
B. I go around the Sun. You live on me.	2. Star
C. I appear to change my shape everyday.	3. Sun
You see me in the sky at night.	4. Moon

(a) A-2, B-3, C-4
(b) A-3, B-1, C-4
(c) A-4, B-2, C-1
(d) A-3, B-1, C-2

57. Which of the following statements is NOT correct about storm? (2021)

(a) It is a slow and gentle moving wind.
(b) It is a fast moving wind that mostly comes with rain and lightning.
(c) It can cause damage to life.
(d) It can cause damage to property.

58. Which of the following statements is correct?

(a) We can see stars shining during the day time.
(b) The Sun gives us light at night.
(c) The Moon gives us light that it gets from the Sun.
(d) The Sun changes its shape everyday.

59. Refer to the given experiment. Ant 1 died before Ant 2. What was the most likely reason? (2022)

(a) Ant 1 did not get air.
(b) Ant 1 did not get food.
(c) Ant 1 did not get water.
(d) Ant 1 did not get both food and water.

60. Solid form of water is called X whereas gaseous form of water is called Y. Select the option that correctly identifies X and Y. **(2022)**

	X	Y
(a)	Steam	Ice
(b)	Steam	Water vapour
(c)	Ice	Breeze
(d)	Ice	Water vapour

RESPONSE GRID

LEVEL 1

1. a b c d	2. a b c d	3. a b c d	4. a b c d	5. a b c d
6. a b c d	7. a b c d	8. a b c d	9. a b c d	10. a b c d
11. a b c d	12. a b c d	13. a b c d	14. a b c d	15. a b c d
16. a b c d	17. a b c d	18. a b c d	19. a b c d	20. a b c d
21. a b c d	22. a b c d	23. a b c d	24. a b c d	25. a b c d
26. a b c d	27. a b c d	28. a b c d	29. a b c d	30. a b c d
31. a b c d	32. a b c d	33. a b c d	34. a b c d	35. a b c d
36. a b c d	37. a b c d	38. a b c d	39. a b c d	40. a b c d
41. a b c d	42. a b c d	43. a b c d	44. a b c d	45. a b c d
46. a b c d	47. a b c d	48. a b c d	49. a b c d	50. a b c d
51. a b c d	52. a b c d	53. a b c d	54. a b c d	55. a b c d
56. a b c d	57. a b c d	58. a b c d		

LEVEL 2

1. a b c d	2. a b c d	3. a b c d	4. a b c d	5. a b c d
6. a b c d	7. a b c d	8. a b c d	9. a b c d	10. a b c d
11. a b c d	12. a b c d	13. a b c d	14. a b c d	15. a b c d
16. a b c d	17. a b c d	18. a b c d	19. a b c d	20. a b c d
21. a b c d	22. a b c d	23. a b c d	24. a b c d	25. a b c d
26. a b c d	27. a b c d	28. a b c d	29. a b c d	30. a b c d
31. a b c d	32. a b c d	33. a b c d	34. a b c d	35. a b c d
36. a b c d	37. a b c d	38. a b c d	39. a b c d	40. a b c d
41. a b c d	42. a b c d	43. a b c d	44. a b c d	45. a b c d
46. a b c d	47. a b c d	48. a b c d	49. a b c d	50. a b c d
51. a b c d	52. a b c d	53. a b c d	54. a b c d	55. a b c d
56. a b c d	57. a b c d	58. a b c d	59. a b c d	60. a b c d

Solutions with Explanations

LEVEL 1

1. (d) In the spring and autumn season, weather is neither hot nor cold.
2. (b) Sun gives us heat & light.
3. (b) Football and tyre-tubes are filled with air.
4. (c) For lighting a fire, we need air.
5. (b) This is due to storm.
6. (b) Cotton clothes are preferred in summer season.
7. (a) We wear raincoat in rainy season
8. (b) The very strong wind with rain or snow is called storm.
9. (c) Raincoat and umbrella are used on a rainy day.
10. (c) Full moon is big and round.
11. (a) Sun rises in the east.
12. (c) Weather keeps changing from day to day.
13. (a)
14. (a) Gumboots are used in rainy days.
15. (b) Weather is not dependent on water.
16. (d) Trees shed their leaves in autumn season.
17. (c) Rainbow is visible in monsoon season.
18. (d)
19. (c) At home we can store water in many ways. Bottles are filled with drinking water and kept in refrigerator. Water is stored in buckets for bathing and washing. Water is also stored in water tank at the top of the house for different uses like drinking, washing, bathing, cleaning, etc.
20. (a) Summer is the hot season whereas, winter is the cold season. Spring season. Spring season is very pleasant, as it is neither too hot nor too cold.
21. (c) 22. (b)
23. (d) The moon appears to change its shape every night. Full moon and new moon are shapes of the moon, but old Moon is not a shape of the moon.
24. (d)
25. (d) Water, soil and sky are not needed for burning but air is needed for burning. Air is always around us. Though we cannot see air but we can feel it. In the absence of air, we cannot light a fire.
26. (d) 27. (d)
28. (a) The moon changes its shape everyday. Some times moon looks round like a ball. It is called a full moon.
29. (d) All living things breath air to stay alive.
30. (a) Sun looks like a big, yellow ball of fire.
31. (c)

32. (a) Only plant 'A' will remain alive after a week as all the conditions necessary for survival and growth, i.e., air, sunlight, water and soil are avaiable to it.
33. (d) Crescent Moon is the Moon that is less than half illuminated by the Sun as shown in option A and C.
34. (b) We do not need water to comb our hair.
35. (c) Burning of crackers will produce smoke and harmful gases which will pollute air around us. Throwing factory vastes in river will pollute water not air.
36. (c) The characteristic of air to move in a particular direction helps us to sail boats and fly kites.
37. (c) 38. (d) 39. (d)
40. (a) 41. (d) 42. (a) 43. (b) 44. (a) 45. (d)
46. (c) 47. (d)
48. (b) Sun is the brightest object in night sky.
49. (c) Washing of clothes doesn't require air.
50. (a)
51. (b) The image shown above represent crescent moon.
52. (c) 53. (d)
54. (a) Air occupies space.
55. (c) Constellations.
56. (a) 57. (b) 58. (b)

LEVEL 2

1. (c) Rainbow is visible in rainy season.
2. (d) Moon gives us light at night and Rakesh Sharma is the first Indian to step on it.
3. (c) On Wednesday, morning is sunny and evening is windy.
4. (b) Sun gives heat and light, moon shines at night and stars twinkle in the sky.
5. (d) The Moon appears round in shape on Full Moon night. Hence, Sonu will se a round shape of the Moon.
6. (a) The option A denotes well. There is water under the ground also and we get that water from wells and pumps.
7. (c) We wear cotton clothes in summers, new flowers blossom in spring. Raincoat is used in monsoon and trees shed leaves in autumn.
8. (a) We come f rom school in the afternoon. So Tanvir while returning home from school, will see the Sun, as Moon and Stars are visible only in the night.
9. (c) Stars are very big. They look small because they are very far away. On, some nights, the Moon disappears completely. It is called New Moon. Sun is not the biggest star in universe yet, it is the biggest visible star on Earth, because it is closest to the Earth.
10. (c) Both air and water are modes of transport. Aeroplane, jetplane, helicopter, etc., are means of air transport whereas ship, boat, submarine, etc., are means of water transport. Hence both air and water help in transportaion.

11. (b) feel 12. (c) Moving 13. (a) breeze
14. (b) storm 15. (c) drinking 16. (b) five
17. (c) summer 18. (a) raincoat 19. (c) moon
20. (b) shape
21. (d) First rat died within few minutes due to unavailability of 'X'. Whereas second rat died after seven days due to unavailability of 'Y'. All living organisms need air, water and food to stay alive. Without food they can live for few days, without water they can live for even lesser time but without air they will die within minutes. Hence 'X' could be air and 'Y' could be food.
22. (c) Both Madhu and Ram are correct as they are talking about sunset. At sunset sun appears bigger and bright orange and also appears to move down.
23. (b) Nishant could have faced storm on his way back home, as his eyes were red due to dirt and his hair were dirty and dry. For removing this dirt, he should take bath.
24. (b)
25. (b) When we fill air in the football then it will increase the weight of the football.
26. (d) Statement A and C are false, the sun gives us light in the day and the moon changes its shape everyday.
27. (a) 28. (b) 29. (c)
30. (d) All of these items are filled with air.
31. (b) In winters, days are very cold. We use to wear woollen clothes in winter.
32. (d) All of these activities can save water.
33. (b) Summer days are hot, winter days are cold, a strong wind blows on a windy day, monsoon days are rainy.
34. (d) Both moon and stars are visible at night.
35. (c) Drinking impure water makes us sick.
36. (a) 37. (c) 38. (b) 39. (a) 40. (c) 41. (d)
42. (c) Air is the mixture of many gases.
43. (c) Living things need air to breathe.
44. (b) 45. (d) 46. (b) 47. (c) 48. (c) 49 (a)
50. (d) It is a source of water - POND
It pollutes air- DUST
It is moving air- WIND
It is inflated by air - BALLOON
51 (d)
52 (b) 53 (b) 54 (c) 55 (d) 56. (b)
57. (a) Strom is fast moving wind.
58. (c)
59. (a) Ant 1 get died early because ant 1 did not get air.
60. (d) Ice is a solid form of water and water vapour is a gaseous form.

8 CHAPTER FOREWORD

You all must have gone on a trip. Which means of transport did your parents choose?

Can you recognize the picture given below? Match the picture with their names.

	Pictures	Names
1		Boat
2		Train
3	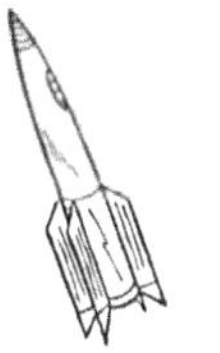	Car
4		Rocket
5		Bicycle

After reading this chapter, you will be able to know about transports in old times and recent times. You will also know about different means of communication.

8 Chapter

Travel and Communication

Real life examples

- Walking and Cycling are good exercises. They do not cause pollution. In many countries people use bicycle instead of cars and motorcycle.

Historical Preview

- Long -long ago people used to travel on animals. People in villages use bullock cart to travel.

LEARNING OBJECTIVES

This lesson will help you to:

- Learn about different means of transport.
- Identify the various means of transport and their importance in daily life.
- Study about communication and identify the various means of communication.

INTRODUCTION

We all move from one place to another for our work, for study etc.

For example, every morning we go to school by school bus. My father goes to office by car. We go to meet our grandparents by train. These all are the means of transport.

MEANS OF TRANSPORT

All the vehicles used for travelling from one place to the other are called means of transport.

There are 3 types of transport: Land, Water and Air.

1. AIR TRANSPORT:
   - Air transport moves in air.
   - It is fastest and most expensive means of transport.
   - For example: Aeroplane, Helicopter.

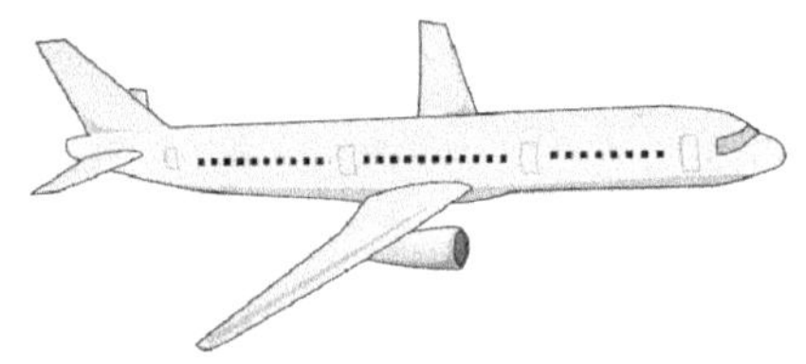

2. WATER TRANSPORT:

- Water transport moves in water.
- These carry people and goods across rivers and seas.
- For example: Boats, Ships, Sailboats.

3. LAND TRANSPORT:

- Land transport moves on land.
- Bicycle, cycle-rickshaws (run by man power); bullock carts, tongas (run by animals); Car, bus, truck, train etc. (run by petrol or diesel or gas engines)

COMMUNICATION

My grandmother lives in Delhi. I talk to her over the telephone. My aunt lives in London, we use to talk to her through computer using internet. We can see her also on the computer. People use different methods to communicate with their friends, family and relatives.

Communication means to speak, write and share ideas and information with each other.

There are different methods by which we can talk to each other. Let us study types of communication in detail.

> **Did You Know?**
>
> ❖ India has one of the largest postal service networks in the world.

TYPES OF COMMUNICATION

1. **Postal Communication:** Post card, Inland letters stamped envelops are means of postal communication.

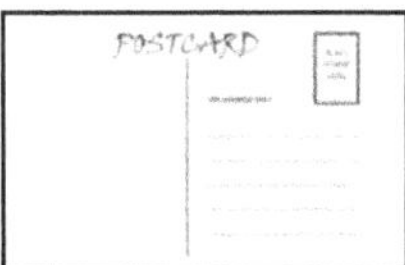

2. **Mass communication:** Newspaper, magazines, radio, television and internet are the example of mass communication.

3. **Modern means of communication:** These are the fastest means of communication.Telephone, mobile phone, e-mail, fax are the example of modern means of communication.

Multiple Choice Questions

LEVEL- 1

1. **Travel means to __________ from one place to another**
   (a) move (b) eat (c) drink (d) all of these
2. **Which of the following is a land transport?**
   (a) Train (b) Aeroplane (c) Ship (d) Boat
3. **Which of the following is a means of transport?**
   (a) Aeroplane (b) Train
   (c) Tiger (d) Both (a) and (b)
4. **We use to come to school by_________.**
   (a) bus (b) train (c) ship (d) aeroplane
5. **Which of the following is the most expensive means of transport?**
   (a) Car (b) Truck (c) Aeroplane (d) Train
6. **Which of the following transport is/are run by animals?** **[Tricky]**
   (a) Bullock cart (b) Ship
   (c) Tongas (d) Both (a) and (c)
7. **Which of the following is the fastest means of transport?**
   (a) Boat (b) Helicopter (c) Bus (d) Train
8. **Which of the following is the fastest means of communication?**
   (a) Letter (b) Telephone
   (c) E-mail (d) Both (b) and (c)
9. **Which of the following is a means of mass communication?** **[Tricky]**
   (a) Newspaper (b) Radio (c) Internet (d) All of these
10. **Which of the following transport runs on petrol?**
    (a) Car (b) Boat
    (c) Truck (d) Both (a) and (c)
11. **Which of the following moves in air?**
    (a) Car (b) Bus (c) Truck (d) Jet plane
12. **Which of the following is a 'Postal means of communication'?** **[Tricky]**
    (a) Post card (b) E-mail
    (c) Fax (d) All of these

13. **Which of the following transport is run by manpower?** **[Tricky]**
    (a) Ship (b) Rickshaw (c) Aeroplane (d) Car

14. **I can fly in the sky. Identify me.**
    (a) Ship (b) Car (c) Helicopter (d) Bus

15. **Telephones are used to**
    (a) talk to a person.
    (b) write letter to a person.
    (c) send a letter to a person.
    (d) none of these.

16. **Which of the following is a modern means of communication?** **[Tricky]**
    (a) Radio (b) Post card (c) E-mail (d) Magazine

17. **Which of the following is the slowest means of communication.**
    (a) Post card (b) Newspaper (c) E-mail (d) Radio

18. **Why we travel?**
    (a) To visit doctor (b) To meet relatives
    (c) To go to school (d) All of these

19. **Heavy and bulky goods are transported by ________?**
    (a) Trolley (b) Bus (c) Truck (d) Boat

20. **Which of the following means of transport moves in water?**
    (a) Ship (b) Steamer (c) Sailboat (d) All of these

21. **Which of the following is the type of mass communication?**
    (a) Newspaper (b) Internet (c) Postcard (d) Both (a) and (b)

22. **Select the INCORRECT match.** **(Critical Thinking)**
    (a) Urgent messages - Letters
    (b) Telephone - STD, ISD
    (c) Internet - E-mail
    (d) Picture news - TV

23. **A ________ carries a message more quickly than a _________. You can talk to the person directly.** **[Tricky]**
    (a) Fax, Telegram (b) Fax, Telephone
    (c) Telephone, Telegram (d) Email, Fax

24. **Which of the following is correct regarding means of mass communication?** **[Tricky]**

(a) It is a postal means of communication.

(b) Radio and television are its example.

(c) It is the slowest means of transport.

(d) None of these.

25. Which of the following means of transport is more expensive?

(a) A.C Bus (b) Aeroplane

(c) Super fast train (d) Car

26. Trains run on railway tracks, so they are called________.

(a) Lod Transport (b) Airways

(c) Railways (d) None of these

27. Consider the following statement and choose the correct option.

Statement A: Water transport is the fastest means of transport.

Statement B: Newspaper, Radio and Television are the means of mass communication.

(a) Statement 'A' is true, statement 'B' is false.

(b) Statement 'B' is true, statement 'A' is false.

(c) Both the statements are true.

(d) Both the statements are false.

28. Identify 'X' and 'Y'. **[Critical Thinking]**

Air transport	**Helicopter**	**'X'**
Mass Communication	'Y'	Newspaper

(a) X = Helicopter, Y = Fax (b) X = Helicopter, Y = E-mail

(c) X = Aeroplane, Y = Radio (d) X = Radio, Y = Television

29. Which of the following can't be used by people to travel from one place to another?

(a) Train (b) Auto rickshaw (c) Scooter (d) Police van

30. Which of the following is the form of air transport? **(2019)**

(a) car (b) Boat (c) Bicycle (d) Helicopter

31. Which of the following vehicle has three wheels? **(2018)**

(a) Auto rickshaw (b) motor bike (c) Cycle (d) Car

LEVEL-2

Direction (Qs. 1 to 5): Find the odd one out. **[Critical Thinking]**

1. (a) Air (b) Water (c) Land (d) Sand
2. (a) Newspaper (b) Radio (c) E-mail (d) Television
3. (a) Car (b) Bus (c) Sailboat (d) Truck
4. (a) Tongas (b) Ship (c) Steamers (d) Boat
5. (a) Telephone (b) Fax (c) E-mail (d) Radio
6. **Rama's grandmother lives alone in her village. None of her children go to meet her. She feels lonely and cries many times. How can Rama interact with her grandmother daily so that her grandmother doesn't feel lonely?**
   (a) Use aeroplane to meet her daily
   (b) Send postcard to her grandmom
   (c) Use telephone/mobile to talk to her daily
   (d) All of these
7. **Which of the following are known as pleasure rides by using flight technology**
   (a) Hot air balloon (b) Blimp **[Tricky]**
   (c) Airplane (d) Both (a) and (b)
8. **Which one of the following is most important in communication?**
   (a) Language (b) Sound
   (c) Telephone (d) None of these

Directions (Qs. 9 to 18): Fill in the blanks in the passage given below.

[Critical Thinking]

We use different types of vehicles to move from one place to another. These are known as means of ____(9)____. There are ____(10)____ types of transport. Air transport moves in____(11)____. It is the ____(12)____ means of transport. Aeroplane and ____(13)____ are the example of air transport. Water transport moves in water. For example Ships and ____(14)____. Land transport moves on land. Bicycle, car, tongas, bus, truck etc. are the examples of ____(15)____ transport. Car, bus and ____(16)____ run on petrol or diesel. Some land transport runs with the help of ____(17)____. For example ____(18)____ and tongas are pulled with help of animals.

9. (a) transport (b) airport
   (c) communication (d) None of these
10. (a) one (b) two
    (c) three (d) four
11. (a) air (b) water
    (c) land (d) sand

12. (a) slowest (b) fastest
(c) cheapest (d) largest
13. (a) sailboat (b) submarine
(c) helicopter (d) train
14. (a) goat (b) boat
(c) road (d) none of these
15. (a) land (b) air
(c) water (d) ocean
16. (a) ship (b) truck
(c) aeroplane (d) All of these
17. (a) plant (b) animals
(c) birds (d) air
18. (a) bullock cart (b) ship
(c) train (d) bus

Directions (Qs. 19-23): Refer the following picture and answer the following questions.

[Critical Thinking]

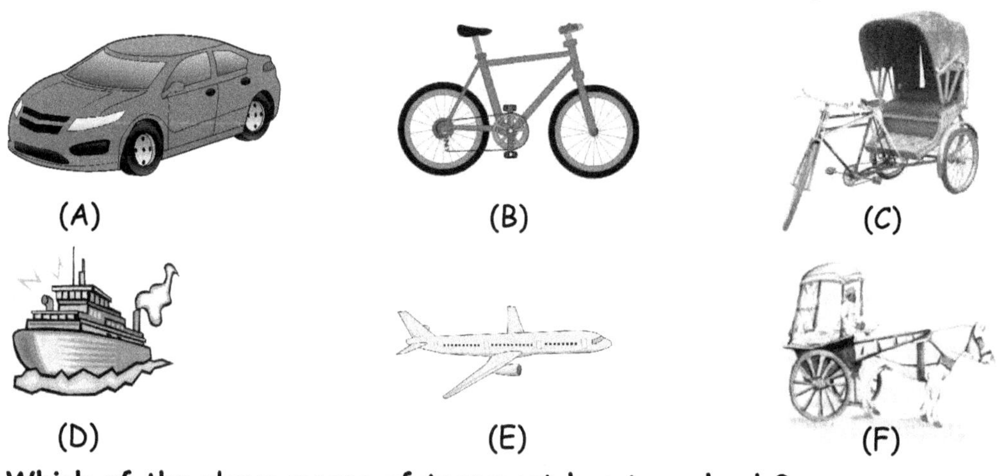

19. **Which of the above means of transport has two wheels?**
(a) Only B (b) Both B and F
(c) Both A and D (d) All of the above
20. **Among which of the above transport can we travel maximum distance in a minimum time?**
(a) A (b) E (c) F (d) D
21. **Which of the above means of transport runs in water?**
(a) A (b) B (c) D (d) F
22. **Which of the above is run by gas engine?**
(a) A (b) C (c) D (d) F
23. **Which of the above is the most expensive means of transport?**
(a) A (b) C (c) D (d) E

RESPONSE GRID

LEVEL 1

1. a b c d	2. a b c d	3. a b c d	4. a b c d	5. a b c d
6. a b c d	7. a b c d	8. a b c d	9. a b c d	10. a b c d
11. a b c d	12. a b c d	13. a b c d	14. a b c d	15. a b c d
16. a b c d	17. a b c d	18. a b c d	19. a b c d	20. a b c d
21. a b c d	22. a b c d	23. a b c d	24. a b c d	25. a b c d
26. a b c d	27. a b c d	28. a b c d	29. a b c d	30. a b c d
31. a b c d				

LEVEL 2

1. a b c d	2. a b c d	3. a b c d	4. a b c d	5. a b c d
6. a b c d	7. a b c d	8. a b c d	9. a b c d	10. a b c d
11. a b c d	12. a b c d	13. a b c d	14. a b c d	15. a b c d
16. a b c d	17. a b c d	18. a b c d	19. a b c d	20. a b c d
21. a b c d	22. a b c d	23. a b c d		

Solutions with Explanation

LEVEL- 1

1. **(a)** Travel means to move from one place to another.
2. **(a)** Train is a land transport. Boat and ship are water transport and aeroplane is an air transport.
3. **(d)** Aeroplane & Train both are the means of transport.
4. **(a)** We come school by bus.
5. **(c)** Aeroplane is the most expensive means of transport.
6. **(d)** Bullock carts and tongas both are run by animals.
7. **(b)** Helicopter is the fastest means of transport.
8. **(d)** Telephone and e-mail both are the fastest means of communication.
9. **(d)** Newspaper, radio, internet all are the means of mass communication.
10. **(a)** Car runs on petrol. Truck runs on diesel.
11. **(d)** Jetplane moves in air.
12. **(a)** Post card is the postal means of communication.
13. **(b)** Rickshaw is run by manpower.
14. **(c)** Helicopter can fly in the sky.
15. **(a)** Telephones are used to talk to a person.

16. (c) E-mail is a modern means of communication.
17. (a) Postcard is the slowest means of communication.
18. (d) We travel to visit doctor, meet relative and go to school.
19. (c) Truck is used for transporting heavy and bulky goods.
20. (d) Ship, steamer and sailboat all are the means of transport that move in water.
21. (d)
22. (a) Urgent messages are sent through e-mail, fax and telephones.
23. (c) A telephone carries a message more quickly than a telegram.
24. (b) Radio and television are the means of mass communication.
25. (b) Aeroplane is the more expensive means of transport.
26. (c) Trains run on railway tracks so they are called Railways.
27. (b) Air transport is the fastest means of transport.
28. (c) 'X' is Aeroplane and 'Y' is Radio which is a Mass communication.
29. (d) Police van is used by police it is not a public transport.
30. (d) Helicopter is a form of air transport while car and bicycle are means of road transport while car and bicycle are road transport. Boat is a means of water transport
31. (a) Auto rickshaw has three wheels. Bike and cycle has two wheels. Car has four wheels

LEVEL- 2

1. (d) Sand is not a means of transport, all others (air, water and land) are the means of transport.
2. (c) E-mail is not a means of mass communication. Newspaper, radio and television all are the means of mass communication.
3. (c) Sailboat is a water transport. Car, bus and truck are land transport.
4. (a) Tongas run by animals. Ship, steamers and boat are water transport.
5. (d) Radio is a means of mass communication. Telephone, fax and e-mail are the modern and fastest means of transport.
6. (c) Rama can use telephone/mobile phone to talk to her grandmom daily as telephone is the fastest means of communication.
7. (d) 8. (a)

9. (a) transport	10. (c) Three	11. (a) air
12. (b) fastest	13. (c) Helicopter	14. (b) boats
15. (a) land	16. (d)	17. (b) animals

18. (a) bullock cart
19. (b) Only bicycle has two wheels.
20. (b) Aeroplane is used to travel maximum distance in minimum time.
21. (c) Ships run in water.
22. (a) Car runs by gas engine as well.
23. (d) Aeroplane is the most expensive means of transport.

CHAPTER FOREWORD

You should understand that throwing waste in the dustbin is a good habit. It helps in recycling the waste. You can make your own dustbin.

Let us learn to make a paper dustbin.

You will need:

Sheets of A4 paper

Method

1. Take a A4 sheet of paper.
2. Fold it along the centre.
3. Then fold it in half again.
4. Take one of the corners and flatten it to make a triangle.
5. Repeat on the other side.
6. Then rotate it and flatten it the other way.
7. Fold one side into the centre. Then the other side.
8. Then again all the way round.
9. Fold the bottom up. And on the other side.
10. Flip it upside-down, stick your hand in and push it out.
11. Your paper dustbin is READY!

After reading this chapter, you will have knowledge about basic types of materials and their uses. you will also be able to learn about recyclable and non-recyclable materials.

9 Chapter

Types of Materials

Did You Know?

❖ It takes 450 years for plastic to begin decomposing and then up to another 80 for it to disappear completely. Every piece of plastic ever made, has still not even began to decompose.

LEARNING OBJECTIVES

This lesson will help you to:

❖ learn about different types of material.

❖ study the characteristics of different materials.

❖ know about the different objects made from these materials.

❖ learn about recyclable and non-recyclable materials.

❖ study about transparent and opaque materials.

INTRODUCTION

We see different objects around us. For example: Table, Chairs, Bottles, Wall-clock, Bags etc. All these objects are made up of different types of materials.

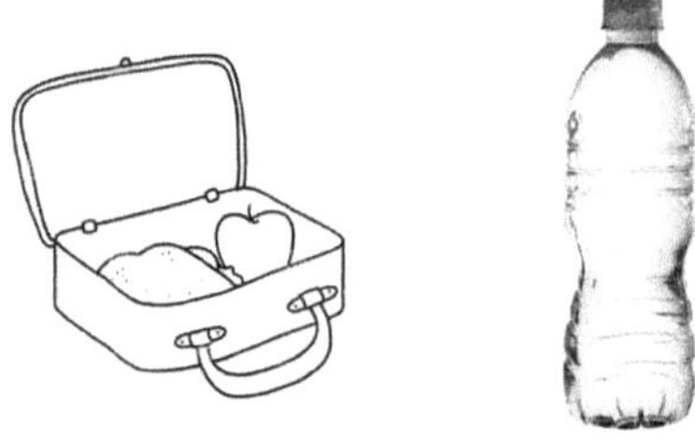

Let us study these materials and their uses:

(1) **Plastic:** Plastic is a material that is used to make water bottles, lunch box, toys, pencil box, buckets, spoons, plates, bowls etc.

Plastic does not breaks easily.

(2) **Wood:** We get wood from trees. Wood is very hard. Wood is used to make tables, chairs, furniture, doors, windows etc.

(3) **Metal:** Metal is a very hard material which doesnot breaks easily.

Metal is used to make different materials like knife, spoon, bicycle, pan, television etc.

(4) **Rubber:** Rubber is obtained from Rubber tree.

Rubber is used to make tyres, eraser, balloon etc.

(5) **Glass:** Glass is a solid material which is used to make sunglasses, mirror, wall-clock, windows etc. Glass can break easily. Glass can easily pass light through them.

TYPES OF OBJECTS

Those objects which allow light to pass through them are called **transparent objects**. For example, Glass etc.

The objects which allow light to pass through them partially are called **translucent objects.** For example, frosted window glass etc.

The objects which do not allow light to pass through them are called **opaque objects**. For example, wood, metal, plastic etc.

RECYCLABLE AND NON RECYCLABLE MATERIAL

Some of the materials can be used again and again by the process of recycling the waste material into new products.

(1) **Recyclable materials** are the materials that can be recycled to become new product. For example: paper, glass, metal, plastic etc.

(2) **Non-recyclable materials** are the materials that can only be used once. They cannot be reused again and again. For example: Coal, petrol etc.

Multiple Choice Questions

LEVEL 1

1. **The frame of Sunglasses is made up of ________.**
   (a) Metal
   (b) Paper
   (c) Wood
   (d) Glass

2. **Which of the following material cannot be recycled?**
   (a) Rubber (b) Coal (c) Paper (d) Plastic

3. **Which of the following materials cannot be used again? [Tricky]**
   (a) Recyclable (b) Non-recyclable
   (c) Reusable (d) None of these

4. **Which of the following object should be crushed after use? [2012, Tricky]**
   (a) Wooden Table
   (b) Plastic Bottle
   (c) Coal
   (d) Eraser

5. **Which of the following can break easily? [Tricky]**
   (a) Wood (b) Plastic (c) Metal (d) Glass

6. **is made up of?**
   WATER
   (a) Paper (b) Wood (c) Plastic (d) None of these

7. **Which of the following is a transparent object?**
   (a) Water (b) Air (c) Glass window (d) All of these

8. **We get wood from ________.**
   (a) animals (b) trees
   (c) glass (d) none of these

9. is made up of?

(a) rubber (b) plastic (c) metal (d) both (b) and (c)

10. **Which of the following can pass light through them?** **[2014, Tricky]**

(a) Wood (b) Metal (c) Glass (d) None of these

11. **Almirah can be made by __________.**

(a) Metal (b) Wood (c) Paper (d) Both (a) and (b)

12. **Objects like wood, rubber & metals are known as __________ as they don't allow ____________ to passs** **[Tricky]**

(a) Transparent, Water (b) Opaque, Light

(c) Translucent, Air (d) Transparent, Air

13. **Which of the following material can be used again?** **[2013, Tricky]**

(a) Coal (b) Petrol (c) Paper (d) Both (a) and (c)

14. **Glass window is _____**

(a) Transparent (b) opaque (c) Translucent (d) None of these

15. **Butter paper is _______**

(a) Oily (b) Transparent (c) Opaque (d) Translucent

16. **Find the odd one out.** **[Tricky]**

(a) Wood (b) Metal (c) Plastic (d) Glass

17. **Which of the following is a substance through which things are partially visible?**

(a) Opaque (b) Translucent

(c) Transparent (d) None of these

18. __________ is the shortest and ___________ is the longest item in the given figure. **(2019)**

(a) Eraser, Marker (b) Pen, Marker

(c) Pen, Eraser (d) Eraser, Pen

19. **In which of the following rooms of the house will you find the objects shown in the given box?** **(2021)**

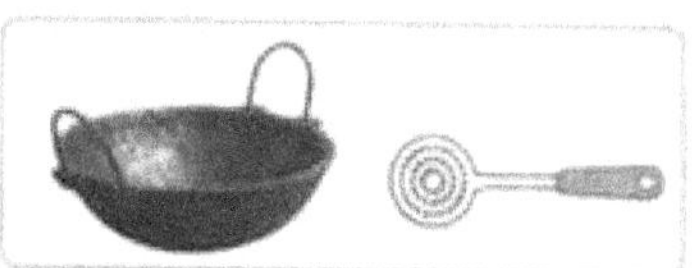

(a) Bedroom (b) Bathroom (c) Living room (d) Kitchen

20. Which of the following tools is used by a farmer? (2021)

(a)  (b)  (c)  (d) 

21. The objects shown in the given picture are commonly found in the _____. (2022)

(a) Bathroom (b) Bedroom (c) Kitchen (d) Living room

22. At the place shown in the given picture you CANNOT ______. (2022)

(a) Buy stamps

(b) Post letters

(c) Send packages

(d) Buy vegetables

23. Match the shapes in column I to the objects given in column II to be drawn with shapes in column I. (2022)

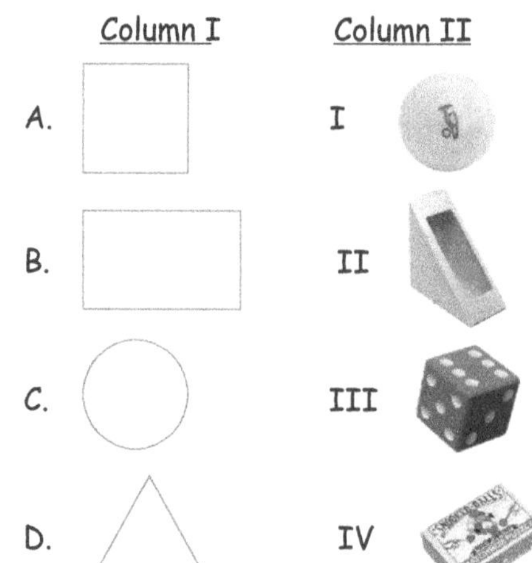

(a) A → IV, B → II, C → I, D → III (b) A → III, B → IV, C → II, D → I

(c) A → III, B → II, C → IV, D → I (d) A → III, B → IV, C → I, D → II

LEVEL 2

Directions (Qs. 1 to 10): Fill in the blanks in the passage given below.

[Critical Thinking]

There are many objects that we see in our day to day life. Each object is made up of different materials. ____(1)____ is used to make buckets, water bottles. It never ____(2)____easily.____(3)____ is obtained from trees that are used to make ____(4)____, tables, chairs etc. Metal is very ____(5)____ that does not easily ____(6)____ and is used to make ____(7)____ , Spoon, Knife etc. Rubber is used to make ____(8)____ of cars, truck, buses. ____(9)____ can break easily. It can pass light through them but ____(10)____ cannot pass light through them.

1. (a) Wood (b) Plastic (c) Metal (d) Glass
2. (a) dissolves (b) breaks (c) smells (d) none of these
3. (a) Wood (b) Plastic (c) Metal (d) Glass
4. (a) glass (b) door (c) bucket (d) toys
5. (a) rubber (b) soft (c) hard (d) both (a) & (b)
6. (a) cut (b) breaks (c) grows (d) plays
7. (a) window (b) door (c) pan (d) All of these
8. (a) door (b) tyre (c) handles (d) window
9. (a) Glass (b) Wood (c) Plastic (d) All of these
10. (a) Glass (b) Metal (c) Wood (d) both (b) & (c)

Directions (Qs. 11 to 16): Find the odd one out. **[Tricky]**

11. (a) Chair (b) Table (c) Door (d) Spoon
12. (a) Glass (b) Plastic (c) Metal (d) Wood
13. (a) Bucket (b) Pencil box (c) Bottle (d) Knife
14. (a) Plastic (b) Coal (c) Paper (d) Wood
15. (a) Tyre (b) Eraser (c) Pencil box (d) Balloon
16. **Consider the following statement and choose the correct answer.**

    Statement A: Wood is very hard and used to make chairs, tables and doors.

    Statement B: Plastics can break easily. **[Critical Thinking]**

    (a) Statement A is true, Statement B is false.

    (b) Statement A is false, Statement B is true.

    (c) Both the statements are true.

    (d) Both the statements are false.

17. Identify 'X', 'Y' and 'Z'. **[Tricky]**

Plastic	Bucket	'X'
Metal	'Y'	Spoon
Recyclable materials	'Z'	Plastic

(a) X = bucket, Y = Mirror, Z = Coal
(b) X = Pencil box, Y = Knife, Z = Paper
(c) X = Door, Y = Car, Z = Petrol
(d) X = Bucket, Y = Knife, Z = Paper

18. Match the Column (I) with Column (II). **[2014, Tricky]**

Column I		Column II	
A.	Tyre	1.	Metal
B.	Knife	2.	Wood
C.	Mirror	3.	Rubber
D.	Door	4.	Glass

	A	B	C	D
(a)	3	4	1	2
(b)	1	2	3	4
(c)	2	3	1	4
(d)	3	1	4	2

Direction (Qs. 19 to 22): Read the passage carefully & answer the following questions. **[Critical Thinking]**

There are many types of objects present in my room. All the objects are made up of different material. The doors, tables, chairs of my room are made up of wood which is very hard, it never breaks. The window panes are made up of glass. I can break the glass of window. My mother's sunglasses are also made up of glass.

19. Which of the following object of my room is made up of wood?

(a) Doors (b) Window
(c) Table (d) Both (a) and (c)

20. The window panes of my room are made up of ________.

(a) metal (b) glass (c) plastic (d) paper

21. Which of the following objects of my room can break easily?

(a) Door (b) Books (c) Window (d) Pencil Box

22. My mother's sunglasses are made up of which of the following material?

(a) Paper (b) Plastic
(c) Glass (d) None of these

23. **The petrol which we use in our vehicles is a ________.** **[2015, Tricky]**

(a) recyclable (b) non-recyclable material
(c) reusable material (d) none of these

24. **Mark the correct option.** **[Tricky]**

1. **Wood cannot break.**
2. **Glass can break easily.**
3. **Glass cannot be recycled**

(a) TTF (b) TFT (c) TTT (d) FTF

25. **Which of the following is an opaque as well as recyclable object?**

(a) Glass (b) Wood (c) Metal (d) Both (b) and (c)

26. **Which of the following items is/are hard, never break easily and opaque object?** **[Tricky]**

A B C D

(a) A and B only (b) A and C only (c) A, C and D (d) All of these

27. **Ram and Shyam are best friends. Ram used to throw the waste papers, plastic bottles etc. outside his door but Shyam used to throw them in the dustbin of his colony's park. According to you, why did Shyam throw these items in the dustbin.**

(a) Because paper and plastic is very costly.
(b) Because paper and plastic is not easily available.
(c) Because paper and plastic can be recycled.
(d) All of these.

28. **My teacher advices us to use the non-recyclable object such as coal, petrol etc. wisely. What do you think is the reason behind this?** **[Tricky]**

(a) They are in limited quantity. (b) They cannot be recycled.
(c) They take time to form. (d) All of these.

29. **Your grandmother has plants in her kitchen. They need lots of light. What type of window should she have install which will be best for her indoor garden?** **[Tricky]**

(a) opaque windows (b) translucent windows
(c) transparent windows (d) no windows, just walls

Directions (Qs. 30 to 39): How much do you know about various types of materials? Apply your knowledge and choose the correct option. Mark your options in the response grid. [Critical Thinking]

30. Candles are made from?

(a) Wood (b) Rubber

(c) Wax (d) Glass

31. Envelops are usually made from?

(a) Paper (b) Rubber

(c) Wax (d) Clay

32. Pots are usually made from?

(a) Leather (b) Rubber

(c) Wax (d) Clay

33. Clothes are usually made from?

(a) Paper (b) Fabric

(c) Glass (d) Wax

34. Tyres are usually made from?

(a) Wood (b) Rubber

(c) Wax (d) Glass

35. Lunch boxes are usually made from ?

(a) Plastic (b) Leather

(c) Glass (d) Wood

36. Shoes are often made from?

(a) Paper (b) Wood

(c) Leather (d) Glass

37. Windows are usually made from?

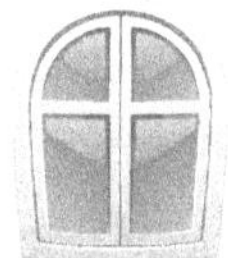

(a) Paper (b) Rubber

(c) Wax (d) Glass

38. Spoons are usually made from?

(a) Fabric (b) Metal

(c) Wax (d) Leather

39. Chairs are often made from?

(a) Wood (b) Paper

(c) Wax (d) Glass

40. Study the given flow chart carefully. Which of the following could be classified under groups X and Y? **(2018)**

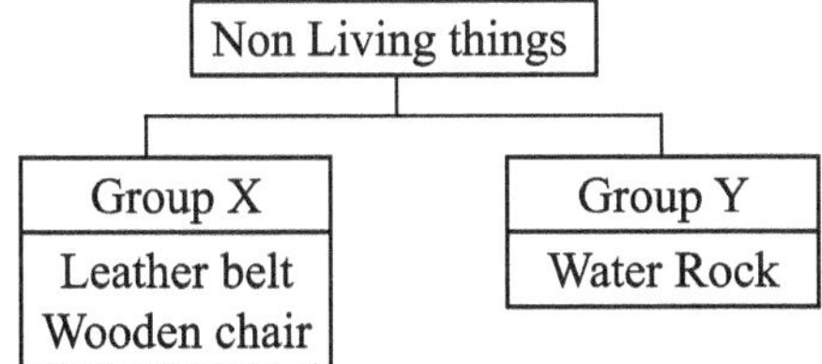

	X	Y
(a)	Frog	Air
(b)	Coconut	Silk saree
(c)	Silver coin	Newspaper
(d)	Cotton frock	Sun

RESPONSE GRID

LEVEL 1

1. a b c d	2. a b c d	3. a b c d	4. a b c d	5. a b c d
6. a b c d	7. a b c d	8. a b c d	9. a b c d	10. a b c d
11. a b c d	12. a b c d	13. a b c d	14. a b c d	15. a b c d
16. a b c d	17. a b c d	18. a b c d	19. a b c d	20. a b c d
21. a b c d	22. a b c d	23. a b c d		

LEVEL 2

1. a b c d	2. a b c d	3. a b c d	4. a b c d	5. a b c d
6. a b c d	7. a b c d	8. a b c d	9. a b c d	10. a b c d
11. a b c d	12. a b c d	13. a b c d	14. a b c d	15. a b c d
16. a b c d	17. a b c d	18. a b c d	19. a b c d	20. a b c d
21. a b c d	22. a b c d	23. a b c d	24. a b c d	25. a b c d
26. a b c d	27. a b c d	28. a b c d	29. a b c d	30. a b c d
31. a b c d	32. a b c d	33. a b c d	34. a b c d	35. a b c d
36. a b c d	37. a b c d	38. a b c d	39. a b c d	40. a b c d

Solutions with Explanations

LEVEL- 1

1. **(a)** The frames of Sunglasses are made up of metal.

2. **(b)** Coal cannot be recycled.

3. (b) Non-recyclable materials cannot be used again.
4. (b) Plastic bottles should be crushed after use.
5. (d) Glass can break easily.
6. (c)
7. (d) Water, air and window are the examples of transparent object.
8. (b) We get wood from trees.
9. (c)
10. (c) Glass can pass light through them.
11. (d) Almirah can be made by both metal and wood.
12. (b) Wood and Rubber are Opaque objects they don't allow light to pass through them.
13. (c) Paper is a recyclable material and thus can be used again.
14. (a) Glass window is a transparent object.
15. (d)
16. (d) Wood, metal and plastic are opaque objects while glass is a transparent object.
17. (b)
18. (a) Eraser is the shortest and Marker is the longest.
19. (d) Items shown are found in kitchen.
20. (a)
21. (c) Microwave, mixers are commonly found in kitchen.
22. (d) At post offices, we cannot buy vegetables.
23. (d) a. Dice is shape of square (iii)
b. Match box is shape of rectangle (iv)
c. Ball is shape of circle (i)
d. Sandwich is shape of triangle (ii)

LEVEL- 2

1. (b) Plastic
2. (b) breaks
3. (a) wood

4. (b) door
5. (c) hard
6. (b) breaks
7. (c) Pan
8. (b) tyres
9. (a) Glass
10. (d) both (b) and (c)
11. (d) Spoon is made up of metal or plastic. Table, chair and door are made up of wood.
12. (a) Glass is a transparent object. Plastic, metal and wood are opaque objects.
13. (d) Knife is made up of metal. Bucket, pencil box and bottle are made up of plastic.
14. (b) Coal is a non-recyclable material. Plastic, paper and wood are recyclable materials.
15. (c) Pencil Box is made up of plastic. Tyres, eraser and balloon are made up of rubber.
16. (a) Wood is very hard and used to make chair, tables and doors. Plastic cannot break easily.
17. (b) 'X' is Pencil box which is made up of plastic. 'Y' is knife which is made up of metal and 'Z' is paper which is a recyclable material.
18. (d) Tyre is made up of rubber. Knife is made up of metal. Mirror is made up of glass and doors are made up of wood.
19. (d) Both doors and tables of my room are made up of wood.
20. (b) The window panes of my room are made up of glass.
21. (c) Window is made up of glass which can break easily.
22. (c) Sunglasses are made up of glass.
23. (b) Petrol is a non-recyclable material.
24. (d) Wood can break, glass can break easily and glass can be recycled.
25. (d) Wood and metal both are opaque as well as recyclable object.
26. (c) Wood, paper and plastic bottle are hard, never break easily and are opaque object.

27. **(c)** Shyam use to throw the waste paper in the dustbin so that these can be recycled.

28. **(d)** Non-recyclable objects are available in limited quantity, they cannot be recycled and take time to form.

29. **(c)** Transparent windows are the best option for her indoor garden.

30. **(c)**	**31.** **(a)**	**32.** **(d)**	**33.** **(b)**
34. **(b)**	**35.** **(a)**	**36.** **(c)**	**37.** **(d)**
38. **(b)**	**39.** **(a)**	**40.** **(d)**	

10 CHAPTER FOREWORD

Festival time is celebration time. You all enjoy to celebrate festivals with your family and friends. You dress up well, eat tasty foods and do fun-filled activities.

Tick the activity that you feel you can do and place a cross against the one you cannot do as part of your contribution to the celebrations of festivals.

I can help to clean my home.	
I can help to clean my neighbourhood.	
I can ask people to use herbal colours during Holi.	
I can ask people not to burst crackers during a festival.	
I can plant a tree in my colony with the help of my friends and look after it.	
I can donate my old clothes to poor people.	
I can cook special food for the festival.	
I can donate my old toys to poor children.	

After reading this chapter, you will appreciate the importance of festivals. You will also know about our national festivals.

10 Chapter

Festivals and Occasions

Historical Preview

- Sikhs also celebrate Diwali, as it marks the release of their guruji-Guru Hargobind Sahibji and 52 other kings and princess of India that were made captives by the mughal emperor Shah Jahan.

Real Life Examples

- People burn crackers on Diwali.

- A Muslim praying Namaz

LEARNING OBJECTIVES

This lesson will help you to:

- Know about different types of occasions.
- Learn about the different types of festivals celebrated in India.
- Understand the importance of national festivals of India.

INTRODUCTION

We all use to celebrate Diwali and Holi together with our brothers, sisters, cousins and friends. Celebrating festivals with our family and friends is a great fun. Let us study about different festivals in detail.

(1) **Diwali:** Diwali is the festival of light. People decorate their houses with candles and do Lakshmi Puja at night. Children burn crackers in the night. Diwali is also known as "Deepavali" which means rows of light.

(2) **Holi:** Holi is the festival of colours. People put 'gulal' and throw coloured water on one another.

(3) **Eid:** Eid is celebrated by Muslims. They do prayer called 'namaaz'. They prepare 'meethi sewaian' for their guests and friends.

(4) **Raksha Bandhan:** Raksha Bandhan is a festival in which sisters tie 'rakhi' on the arms of their brothers and wish for the health and well being.

(5) **Guruparva:** Guruparva is celebrated by the Sikh. They go to 'Gurudwaras' to pray.

(6) **Christmas:** Christmas is celebrated on 25th December of every year. In this festival, christmas tree is decorated with lights. Children wait for Santa Claus to bring gifts for them.

(7) **Dussehra:** Dussehra is celebrated on the tenth day of Navratra. Ravana, Kumbhkaran and Meghanad get burnt every year on this day.

Amazing Fact

- **Christmas was considered as a pagan festival. In United states, Christmas became a festival in 1840 and was made a public holiday in 1870. The Christmas tree is symbolized as the "Tree of Paradise" being the tree of life.**

Harvesting Festivals: Harvesting festivals of Indian states occurs at the time of main harvest of that region and people. States of India celebrates its own harvest festival at various time throughout the year. Major harvest festivals in India are:

- Onam → January, in Kerala
- Pongal → January, in Kerala
- Lohri → January, in Punjab
- Makar Sankranti → In spring season in all parts of India

We celebrate the birthdays of our family members and attend the wedding of our loved ones. These are all **family occassions**.

NATIONAL FESTIVALS

There are so many festivals celebrated in India. There are three national festivals which we celebrate in India.

(1) **Independence day:** It is celebrated on 15 August every year. The Prime Minister hoists the National Flag at the Red Fort in Delhi.

(2) **Republic Day:** It is celebrated on 26 January every year. The armed forces, folk dancers, and school children in colourful dresses take part in a parade at Rajpath in New Delhi.

(3) **Gandhi Jayanti:** It is celebrated every year on 2nd October. People pay tribute by offering flowers on his samadhi in Rajghat (New Delhi).

Apart from these days, Children's Day is celebrated on 14th November every year on the birthday of Jawaharlal Nehru. Teachers Day is celebrated on 5th September every year on the birthday of Dr. Radhakrishnan.

Historical Preview

- India got independence on 15th August 1947. Before that India was under the rule of British.

Did you Know?

- Kite flying is a very popular game in India. Many people fly kites on 15 August every year to celebrate Independence Day.
- There are also special kite flying festivals celebrated in India.

Did you Know?

- The Lasoong festival is the most popular festival of Sikkim. It is usually celebrated at the end of tenth Tibetan lunar month (usually December). It is one of the important festivals among the Bhutias in India.

Multiple Choice Questions

LEVEL- 1

1. **Which of the following is the festival of light and crackers?**
   (a) Holi (b) Diwali (c) Dussehra (d) Christmas
2. **Rajghat is the samadhi of which of the following national leaders?**
   (a)  (b)  (c)  (d) 
3. **Dussehra is celebrated on ______ day of Navratri.** **[Tricky]**
   (a) 2 (b) 5 (c) 10 (d) 12
4. **'Gulal' and 'Coloured Water' are used on which of the following festival?**
   (a) Holi (b) Diwali (c) Dussehra (d) Eid
5. **What is the prayer of the Muslims called ________.** **[Tricky]**
   (a) aarti (b) namaaz (c) bhajan (d) azaan
6. **Whose birthday is celebrated as the Teachers' Day?** **[2012,Tricky]**
   (a) Dr. Rajendra Prasad (b) Lala Lajpat Rai
   (c) Dr. Radhakrishnan (d) Bal Gangadhar Tilak
7. **In which of the following occasions people use to decorate their house with different lights, diyas etc.?**
   (a) Dussehra (b) Diwali (c) Christmas (d) Holi
8. **Guruparva is celebrated by ___________.**
   (a) Hindus (b) Muslims (c) Sikhs (d) Christmas
9. **Whose birthday is celebrated as "Childrens' Day"?**
   (a) Mahatma Gandhi (b) Dr. Radha Krishnan
   (c) Jesus Christ (d) Pt. Jawaharlal Nehru
10. **Which of the following is a correct match?** **[Tricky]**
    (a) Christmas - Crackers
    (b) Diwali - Lakshmi puja
    (c) Guruparva - Santa Claus
    (d) Dussehra - Colour
11. **Which of the following festivals is celebrated on the same date every year?** **[Tricky]**
    (a) Raksha Bandhan (b) Janmashtami
    (c) Durga Puja (d) Christmas

12. **Which of the following is celebrated on 15th August every year?**
    (a) Independence Day (b) Christmas Day
    (c) Teacher's Day (d) Republic Day
13. **Onam is an important festival celebrated in which state of India? [Tricky]**
    (a) Bihar (b) Kerala
    (c) Delhi (d) Jammu and Kashmir
14. **Which of the following is known as the 'festival of brother-sister'?**
    (a) Diwali (b) Teachers' Day
    (c) Raksha Bandhan (d) Holi
15. **'Meethi Sewaian' is prepared in which of the following festival?**
    (a) Holi (b) Diwali (c) Eid (d) Dussehra
16. **Which of the following is a family occasion?**
    (a) Birthday (b) Wedding
    (c) Holi (d) Both (a) and (b)
17. **Gandhi Jayanti is celebrated on _____.**
    (a) 15 August (b) 26 January
    (c) 2 October (d) None of these
18. **"Lohri" is celebrated in which month?**
    (a) April (b) August (c) January (d) October
19. **Lasoong festival is celebrated in which state of India? [2014, Tricky]**
    (a) Assam (b) Goa (c) Mumbai (d) Sikkim
20. **Which of the following is the National festival of India?**
    (a) Eid (b) Gandhi Jayanti
    (c) Christmas Day (d) Teachers Day
21. **Which one is not a religious festival?**
    (a) Holi (b) Gandhi Jayanti (c) Diwali (d) Good Friday
22. **Which of the following is a harvesting festival? [Tricky]**
    (a) Guruparva (b) Diwali
    (c) Makar Sankranti (d) Eid
23. Which of the following festivals is being celebrated in the picture shown here? **(2019)**
    (a) Religious festival - Festival of lights
    (b) National festival - Gandhi Jayanti
    (c) National festival - Republic Day
    (d) Religious festival - Festival of colours

24. What comes next in the figure pattern shown below? **(2022)**

(a)  (b)  (c)  (d) 

25. Which of the following is a religious festival? **(2022)**

(a) Eid (b) Republic Day

(c) Gandhi Jayanti (d) Independence Day

LEVEL- 2

1. On which of the given festivals we **[Critical Thinking]**

- **put on new dresses**
- **decorate our houses**
- **do worship of Lakshmi ji**

(a) Eid (b) Diwali (c) Christmas (d) All of these

2. The given picture shows which occasion in the family?

(a) Birthday celebrations (b) Anniversary

(c) Wedding (d) Housewarming

3. Who hoists the National Flag on Independence day at Red fort? **[Tricky]**

(a) President (b) Governor

(c) Chief Minister (d) Prime Minister

4. Which of the following is an incorrect match? **[2013, Tricky]**

Column I		Column II	
(a)	Christmas	-	Crackers
(b)	Holi	-	Colours
(c)	Guruparva	-	Gurudwara
(d)	Dussehra	-	Burning of Ravan

5. **Select the INCORRECT statement for Sports Day Celebration.** **[Tricky]**
   (a) We have sports day once a year.
   (b) We win medals and trophies on Sports Day.
   (c) We celebrate Sports Day in public.
   (d) Our parents come along to watch the sports.
6. **Which of the following is TRUE about the given image.**

   (a) It is the festival of colours. (b) People put gulal on one another.
   (c) People prepare 'sewaian'. (d) Both (a) and (b).
7. **Identify the festival being celebrated as shown in the given picture and tell how people celebrate this festival?** **(Critical Thinking)**

   (a) They decorate trees with sweets and toys
   (b) They go to mosque to pray namaaz
   (c) They throw coloured water on one another.
   (d) They tie Rakhi on the arm of one another.
8. **Which of the following statement is true for the Republic Day?** **[Tricky]**
   (1) On 15 August, India became Republic
   (2) On Republic Day, a parade is held in New Delhi on the Rajpath
   (3) The Prime Minister hoists National flag at Red Fort in Delhi
   (a) 1 and 3 (b) 2 and 3 (c) 2 and 4 (d) All of these

9. Consider the following statements and choose the correct option.

Statement A: Teacher's Day is a National festival. **[Critical Thinking]**

Statement B: Eid is celebrated by Muslim.

(a) Statement A is true, Statement B is false.
(b) Statement A is false, Statement B is true.
(c) Both the statements are true.
(d) Both the statements are false.

10. What is the literal meaning of "Deepavali"? **[Tricky]**

(a) Rows of light (b) Coloured lights
(c) Brightness of lights (d) None of these

11. Which of the following national festival fall in August?

(a) Republic Day (b) Teacher's Day
(c) Independence Day (d) Both (a) and (c)

12. Match the Column (I) with Column (II).

Column I		Column II	
A.	Holi	1.	Sculpture of Raavan get burnt
B.	Eid	2.	Meethi sewaian
C.	Dussehra	3.	Colours

	A	B	C
(a)	1	2	3
(b)	3	1	2
(c)	2	1	3
(d)	3	2	1

Direction (Qs. 13 to 22): Fill in the blanks of the given passage. **[Critical Thinking]**

We use to celebrate festivals together with our family. On ____(13)____ we burn crackers and decorate our ____(14)____ . Holi is the festival of____(15)____. Guruparva is celebrated by ____(16)____. They go to ____(17)____ on this day.Eid is celebrated by ____(18)____ . They prepare ____(19)____ for their guests. They do prayer called namaaz. ____(20)____ is celebrated on the tenth day of navratra. Raksha Bandhan is the festival of brother and ____(21)____ . On this day, sisters tie ____(22)____ on the arms of their brothers.

13. (a) Holi (b) Diwali (c) Christmas (d) Teacher's day

14. (a) school (b) hospital (c) houses (d) road

15. (a) candles (b) crackers (c) sewaian (d) colours

16. (a) Sikhs (b) Hindus (c) Muslims (d) Christians
17. (a) temples (b) mosques (c) gurudwaras (d) all of these
18. (a) Hindus (b) Muslims (c) Christians (d) Sikhs
19. (a) sweet (b) sewaian (c) burger (d) all of these
20. (a) Diwali (b) Dussehra (c) Holi (d) Christmas
21. (a) sister (b) father (c) mother (d) friend
22. (a) watch (b) rakhi
(c) Both of these (d) None of these

23. Identify 'X', 'Y' and 'Z'. **[Critical Thinking]**

'X'	Gulal	Coloured Water
Christmas	'Y'	Christmas tree
National Day	Independence Day	'Z'

(a) X = Holi, Y = Sewaian, Z = Eid
(b) X = Holi, Y = Santa Claus, Z = Republic Day
(c) X = Eid, Y = Holi, Z = Teacher's Day
(d) X = Diwali, Y = Santa Claus, Z = Christmas Day

24. Your friend Shivam does not know how Independence Day is celebrated? As a friend what you will tell him about this National Festival?

(a) On National days, we use to burn crackers.
(b) On National days, we use to play with crackers.
(c) On this day, India got independence so our Prime Minister hoists National Flag at the Red Fort.
(d) On this day we go to temple and do prayer.

25. Which of the following thing we should do in festivals and family occasions?

(a) We should celebrate the festivals and occasion by watching T.V and dancing.
(b) We all get together to celebrate the festivals.
(c) We should go to restaurant on festivals.
(d) All of these.

26. Which of the following statement is CORRECT about Dussehra? [2015, Tricky]

(a) We use to go to gurudwara for prayer.
(b) Dussehra is celebrated on the tenth day of Navratra.
(c) We burn the sculpture/dummy of Ravan, Kumbhkaran and Meghanad on this day.
(d) Both (b) and (c)

27. On Pongal people worship________. **(Tricky)**

(a) Moon (b) Crops (c) Sun (d) All of these

28. I am a sweet dish that is made on Eid.

(a) Ladoo (b) Sewaian (c) Jalebi (d) Rassam

Direction (Qs. 29 to 31): Read the following poem carefully and answer the following question. **[Critical Thinking]**

Christmas time was here
Everything was white
Santa Claus comes with gifts
One dark and snowy night
Come and see
The Christmas tree
It is pretty
as can be

29. Which of the following festival is described in the poem.

(a) Diwali (b) Holi (c) Dussehra (d) Christmas

30. In the above poem who comes with gifts?

(a) Teacher (b) Santa Claus (c) Snowman (d) None of these

31. Which of the following is looking beautiful in the above poem?

(a) Santa Claus (b) Christmas tree (c) Snow (d) All of these

32. Identify the festival being celebrated in the given picture and select the correct option. **(2018)**

(a) Independence Day - Prime Minister of India hoists the flag and addresses the nation.

(b) Republic Day - President of India hoists the flag and addresses the nation.

(c) Independence Day- President of India hoists the flag and addresses the nation.

(d) Republic Day - Prime Minister of India hoists the flag and addresses the nation.

33. Complete the following sentences by choosing the correct sequence of words.

(i) We go to a ______ to report a theft in our house. **(2021)**

(ii) Sikhs go to a ______ for offering their prayers.

(a) Post office, Gurdwara (b) Police station, Mosque

(c) Railway station, Church (d) Police station, Gurdwara

RESPONSE GRID

LEVEL 1

1. a b c d	2. a b c d	3. a b c d	4. a b c d	5. a b c d
6. a b c d	7. a b c d	8. a b c d	9. a b c d	10. a b c d
11. a b c d	12. a b c d	13. a b c d	14. a b c d	15. a b c d
16. a b c d	17. a b c d	18. a b c d	19. a b c d	20. a b c d
21. a b c d	22. a b c d	23. a b c d	24. a b c d	25. a b c d

LEVEL 2

1. a b c d	2. a b c d	3. a b c d	4. a b c d	5. a b c d
6. a b c d	7. a b c d	8. a b c d	9. a b c d	10. a b c d
11. a b c d	12. a b c d	13. a b c d	14. a b c d	15. a b c d
16. a b c d	17. a b c d	18. a b c d	19. a b c d	20. a b c d
21. a b c d	22. a b c d	23. a b c d	24. a b c d	25. a b c d
26. a b c d	27. a b c d	28. a b c d	29. a b c d	30. a b c d
31. a b c d	32. a b c d	33. a b c d		

Solutions with Explanation

LEVEL- 1

1. **(b)** Diwali is the festival of light and crackers.
2. **(a)** Rajghat is the samadhi of Mahatama Gandhi.
3. **(c)** Dussehra is celebrated on the 10th day of Navratri.
4. **(a)** Holi is the festival of Gulal and Coloured water.
5. **(b)** The prayer of Muslims is known as 'Namaaz'.
6. **(c)** Dr. Radhakrishnan's birthday is celebrated as Teachers' Day.
7. **(b)** On diwali, we decorate our houses with different diyas, lights etc.
8. **(c)** Guruparva is celebrated by Sikhs.
9. **(d)** "Childrens' Day" is celebrated on 14th November, on the occasion of birthday of Jawaharlal Nehru.
10. **(b)** On Diwali, we do Lakshmi puja.
11. **(d)** Christmas is celebrated on the same date (25th December) every year.

12. (a) Independence Day is celebrated on 15th August every year.

13. (b) Onam is celebrated in Kerala.

14. (c) Raksha Bandhan is the festival of brother and sister.

15. (c) 'Meethi Sewaian' is prepared on Eid.

16. (d) Birthday and wedding both are family occasion.

17. (c) Gandhi Jayanti is celebrated on 2nd October.

18. (c) Lohri is celebrated in the month of January.

19. (d) Lasoong is celebrated in Sikkim.

20. (b) Gandhi Jayanti is the National festival of India.

21. (b) 22. (c) 23. (c)

24. (b) The arrow moving in clockwise direction.

25. (a) Eid

LEVEL- 2

1. (b) The festival described here is Diwali.

2. (c) The given picture shows wedding.

3. (d) The Prime Minister hoists the National Flag on Independence Day.

4. (a) On Diwali, we burn crackers.

5. (c) Sports Day is celebrated in the school playground.

6. (d) Holi is described in the given image. It is the festival of colours and people put gulal on one another.

7. (b) The festival shown in the image is 'Eid'. In this festival, people use to pray namaaz.

8. (b) Statement 2 and Statement 3 are true.

India became independent on 15th August.

Republic Day is celebrated on 26th January.

9. (b) Teachers' Day is not a national festival and Eid is celebrated by Muslims.

10. (a) The literal meaning of "Deepavali" is the rows of lights.

11. (c) Independence day is celebrated on 15th August.

12. (d) Holi is the festival of colours. On Eid we prepare meethi sewaian for our guests. On Dussehra, the effigies of Ravaan get burnt.

13. (b) Diwali

14. (c) houses

15. (d) colours

16. (a) Sikhs

17. (c) gurudwara

18. (b) Muslims

19. (b) Sewaian

20. (b) Dussehra

21. (a) sister

22. (b) rakhi

23. (b) 'X' is Holi which is a festival of gulal and coloured water. 'Y' is Santa Claus and 'Z' is Republic Day which is a National Day.

24. (c) 25. (b) 26. (d) 27. (c)

28. (b)

29. (d) Christmas is described in the poem.

30. (b) In the above poem, Santa Claus comes with gifts.

31. (b) Christmas tree is looking beautiful in the poem.

32. (a) Prime Minister of India hoists the flag at the Red Fort on every Independence Day.

33. (d) We go to Police Station to report theft.

Sikhs go to Gurudwara to offer prayers.

11 CHAPTER FOREWORD

You all want to be something when you grow up. Some of you want to be a sportsman, a lawyer, a doctor, an engineer, pilot, or chef. Different people do different works and help each other in a society.

Choose words from the box given below and fill the blanks.

doctor, police, soldier, farmer, traffic police

- When I am sick or hurt ____________________ gives me medicines to cure me.
- ________________________ makes sure that we obey the traffic rules.
- ________________________ protects my country from enemies.
- ________________________ grows food for people to eat.
- ________________________ catches thieves.

After reading this chapter, you will be able to know more about people and professions. You will also know about farmers, personalities of India and the world.

11

Chapter

Occupation and Famous Personalities

Amazing Facts

❖ Albert Einstein, the world famous scientist suffered from dyslexia. Because of his bad memory he was not able to memorise simple things.

Real Life Examples

❖ A doctor treating his patient

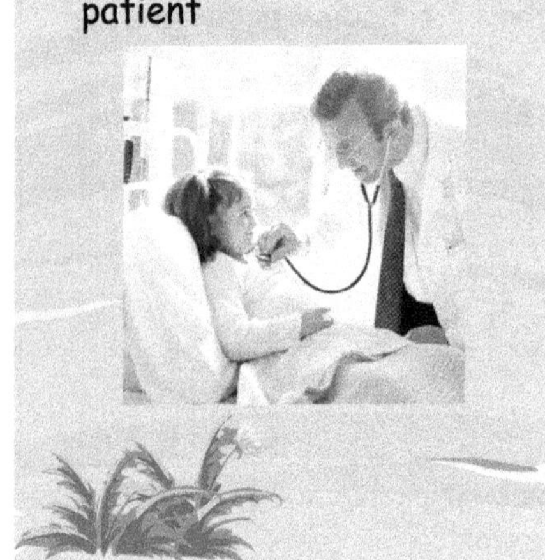

LEARNING OBJECTIVES

This lesson will help you to:

- ❖ Study about different occupations.
- ❖ Learn about the work done by different types of people.
- ❖ Know about the famous personalities of the World.

QUICK CONCEPT REVIEW

We all live in a society. In order to live each person of the society has to do some work. This work gives us money for buying food and clothes. Such work becomes the job. Occupation is the job that a person does. People have different occupations. Let us study these occupation in detail.

1. **Engineer:** An engineer designs and repairs machines, metro rail, roads, etc.

2. **Doctor:** A doctor treats the patients.

3. **Nurse:** A nurse takes care of the sick people.
4. **Soldier :** A soldier is one who fights as a part of an army. He always strives for the safety and security of others. He leaves his family and friends and fight for his country.
5. **Waiter :** A waiter or waitress serves us in the restaurant. They bring our food and give us hospitality. After the dinner or food they bring bill which we pay. They follow the guidelines that are developed by the manager.
6. **Baker :** A baker is someone who will mix and bake ingredients according to recipes to make breads, pastries and other baked goods. These goods are sold by grocers, in restaurants etc.
7. **Pilot :** An aircraft pilot is a person who controls the flight by operating its directional flight controls. Airlines pilots usually work in pairs and responsible for all crew and passengers from boarding to landing.
8. **Chemist:** Chemist sells medicines and injections.
9. **Blacksmith:** A blacksmith repairs things made up of iron.
10. **Farmer:** A farmer grows crops, fruits and vegetables for us.
11. **Postman:** A postman brings letters and parcels.
12. **Tailor:** A tailor stitches our clothes.
13. **Fireman:** A fireman puts water on the fire.
14. **Carpenter:** A carpenter makes and repairs wooden things.
15. **Grocer:** A grocer sells food and other things that are used at home.
16. **Mechanic:** A mechanic repairs our vehicles.
17. **Plumber:** A plumber fits and repairs pipes.
18. **Potter:** A potter makes clay pots for us.
19. **Astronaut:** Astronaut goes to space
20. **Cobbler:** Cobbler repairs our shoes

There are some people such as policeman, pilot, armyman who wear special clothes called uniform.

Nurse Pilot

Tailor

Postman

Farmer

Carpenter

Plumber

Grocer

Historical Preview

❖ Kalpana Chawla was the first Indian-born woman to reach space and the first Indian-American astronaut.

FAMOUS PERSONALITIES OF THE WORLD:

Mother Teresa

1. **Mother Teresa:** Mother Teresa was a Social Worker. She helped old, poor and sick people.

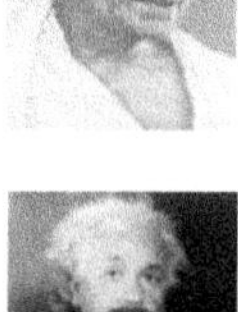

Mahatma Gandhi

2. **Mahatma Gandhi:** Mahatma Gandhi is the father of the nation.

Albert Einstein

3. **Albert Einstein:** Albert Einstein worked in the field of science and technology.

Jawaharlal Nehru

4. **Jawaharlal Nehru:** He was the first Prime Minister of India. He was popularly known as "Chacha Nehru".

Narendra Modi

5. **Narendra Modi:** He is the Prime Minister of India.

Rabindra Nath Tagore

6. **Rabindra Nath Tagore:** He worked in the field of literature and music.

Sania Mirza

7. **Sania Mirza:** Sania Mirza is the famous tennis player of India.

APJ Abdul Kalam

8. **APJ Abdul Kalam:** He was a scientist and former president of India.

Sachin Tendulkar

9. **Sachin Tendulkar:** Sachin Tendulkar is the famous cricketer and former Captain of India.

Barack Obama

10. **Barack Obama:** Barack Obama was the President of America.

Multiple Choice Questions

LEVEL- 1

Directions (Qs. 1 to 15): Choose the correct option from those given below.

1. **Which of the following makes furniture at our home?.**

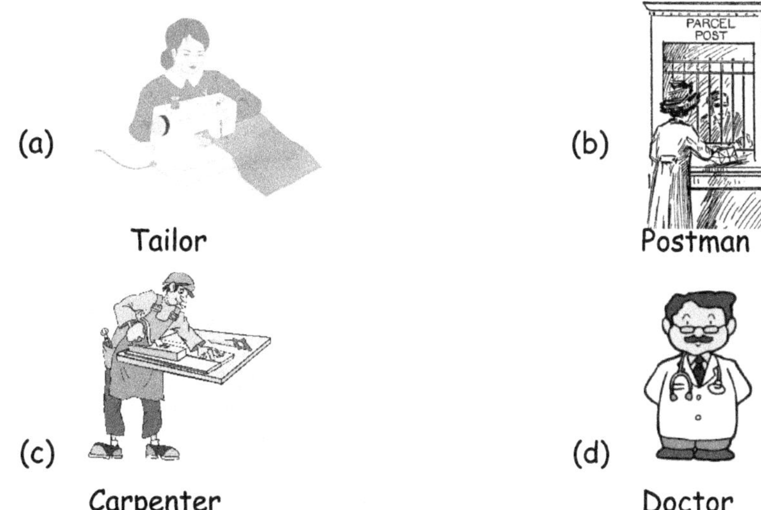

(a) Tailor
(b) Postman
(c) Carpenter
(d) Doctor

2. **The man in the figure is a/an__________.**

(a) Astronaut (b) Sea diver (c) Fire-man (d) Pilot

3. **Fill up the missing alphabets to find out the correct occupation of the man shown in the figure.** **[Tricky]**

① O ② ③ ④ R

(a) D, C, T, E (b) P, S, T, E (c) C, B, L, E (d) P, T, T, E

4. **Madhav is a ________. He use to repair .** **[Tricky]**

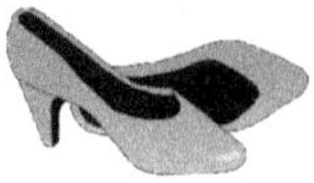

(a) Potter (b) Blacksmith (c) Cobbler (d) Mason

5. **An ________ designs and builds roads, metro rail, bridges, etc.**

(a) Engineer (b) Editor (c) Doctor (d) Astronaut

6. **Which of the following is the famous cricketer of India.**

(a)  Sania Mirza

(b)  Sachin Tendulkar

(c)  Barack Obama

(d)  Albert Einstein

7. **Find the odd one out.** **[Tricky]**

(a) Doctor (b) Nurse (c) Chemist (d) Tailor

8. **Who fits and repairs pipes at our home?** **[2013]**

(a) Potter (b) Plumber

(c) Mechanic (d) None of these

9.  **works in the field of ________.**

(a) Music (b) Science (c) Sports (d) English

10. **Which of the following was the first Prime Minister of India?.**

(a) Mahatma Gandhi (b) Jawahar Lal Nehru

(c) Narendra Modi (d) Barack Obama

11. **Which of the following was a social worker, who helped poor, old and sick people?.**

(a)  Sania Mirza

(b)  Mother Teresa

(c)  Rabindra Nath Tagore

(d)  Barack Obama

12. **Which of the following was the famous scientist and former President of India?** **[Tricky]**

(a) Albert Einstein (b) APJ Abdul Kalam

(c) Rabindra Nath Tagore (d) Barack Obama

13. **I bring you your dinner in a restaurant and after dinner I bring the bill to pay?**

(a) A Cook (b) A Waiter (c) A Teacher (d) Plumber

14. **If you have a problem with your car, I can help to fix it. I am a**

(a) Potter (b) Chemist (c) Mechanic (d) Pilot

15. **I am in the army. I carry a gun.**

(a) A police officer (b) A Doctor (c) A Soldier (d) A Tailor

16. **_________ stitches our clothes.** **[2016]**

(a) Tailor (b) Carpenter

(c) Potter (d) None of these

17. **Who among the following person takes care of the sick person?** **[Tricky]**

(a) Chemist (b) Nurse

(c) Tailor (d) Both (a) and (b)

18. **Who among the following makes and repair things made up of iron?** **[Tricky]**

(a) Plumber (b) Blacksmith (c) Carpenter (d) Potter

19. I am the person who flies an aeroplane.

(a) A Doctor (b) A Teacher (c) A Pilot (d) An Actor

20. Jude felix is a famous Indian player in which of the fields? [2017, Tricky]

(a) Volleyball (b) Tennis (c) Hockey (d) Football

21. ______ was the first Indian to go into the space. [2015]

(a) Rakesh Sharma (b) Kalpana Chawala

(c) Sunita Williams (d) None of these

22. Which of the following is a correct match? **(2019)**

(a) Cobbler - Grows crops

(b) Farmer - Delivers letters

(c) Tailor - Stitches clothes

(d) Postman - Mends shoes

23. ________ was the first Indian woman to go in space. **(2018)**

(a) Mary Kom (b) Kalpana Chawla

(c) Sunita Williams (d) Bachendri Pal

24. A/an ______ fits and repairs taps and pipes. (2021)

(a) Tailor (b) Mason (c) Plumber (d) Electrician

25. Who among the following was the first person to go on the Moon? (2022)

(a) Rakesh Sharma (b) Sunita Williams

(c) Neil Armstrong (d) Kalpana Chawla

26. Refer to the given word chop table. Which of the following sets of boxes will give the name of the person who fits and repairs water pipes and taps? (2022)

1_{DO}	2_{MA}	3_{PL}	4_{CT}
5_{ST}	6_{UM}	7_{SC}	8_{TEA}
9_{HO}	10_{CH}	11_{SON}	12_{BER}
13_{AY}	14_{OL}	15_{ER}	16_{OR}

(a) 2 and 11 (b) 3, 6 and 12 (c) 8, 10 and 15 (d) 1, 4 and 16

27. A place where doctors treat sick people is called: (2022)

(a) Fire station (b) Airport (c) Hospital (d) Kennel

LEVEL- 2

1. Which of the following statements is CORRECT for the given image?

[Tricky]

(a) It helps us to send message from one place to another.

(b) It has an ambulance to carry the letters.

(c) We buy letters and envelopes from here.

(d) Both (a) and (c)

2. Identify the correct match. **[Tricky]**

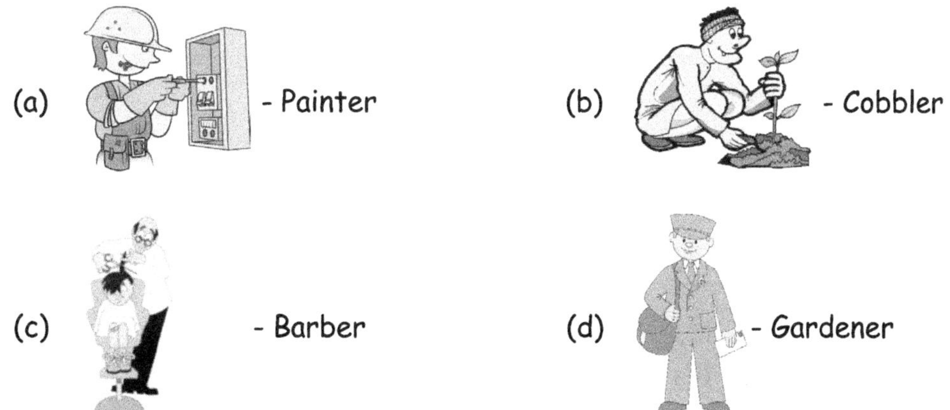

(a) - Painter

(b) - Cobbler

(c) - Barber

(d) - Gardener

3. The person who sells the items shown in the below figure is called __________.

[Tricky]

(a) Chemist (b) Florist (c) Grocer (d) Potter

4. Select the INCORRECT match. **[2012]**

(a)  - Brings letters and parcels.

(b)  - Takes care of the bank

(c)  - Stitches our clothes

(d)  - Fits and repairs pipes and taps

Directions (Qs. 5 - 10): Fill in the blanks in the given passage. (Critical Thinking]

Each one of us has to do some work to earn money which is called job. _____(5)_____ is the job that a person does. Different person do different kinds of work. _____(6)_____ treats the patient. _____(7)_____ take care of the sick patient. A _____(8)_____ brings letters and parcel to us from the post office. A _____(9)_____ makes and repair things made up of iron. A carpenter makes and repairs _____(10)_____ things. **[Critical Thinking]**

5.	(a) Work	(b) Play	(c) Occupation	(d) None of these
6.	(a) Doctor	(b) Nurse	(c) Plumber	(d) Potter
7.	(a) Doctor	(b) Nurse	(c) Tailor	(d) Policeman
8.	(a) plumber	(b) potter	(c) postman	(d) policeman
9.	(a) doctor	(b) blacksmith	(c) potter	(d) carpenter
10.	(a) iron	(b) wooden	(c) fireman	(d) grocer

11. Which of the following statements is 'TRUE' for Doctor?

(a) Gives us medicine when we are sick.

(b) Makes our furniture.

(c) Brings parcel and letter to our home.

(d) Both (a) & (b)

12. Consider the following statement and choose the correct answer.

Statement A: Mother Teresa was a scientist. **[Critical Thinking]**

Statement B: Carpenter stitches our clothes.

(a) Statement A is true, Statement B is false.

(b) Statement A is false, Statement B is true.

(c) Both the statement are true.

(d) Both the statement are false

13. Identify 'X' and 'Y'. **[Tricky]**

Area of Work	Person	
Medicine	'X'	Doctor
Science	Albert Einstein	'Y'

(a) X = Postman, Y = Mother Teresa

(b) X = Nurse, Y = Rabindra Nath Tagore

(c) X = Plumber, Y = Sachin Tendulkar

(d) X = Chemist, Y = APJ Abdul Kalam

14. Read the statements made by four children. **[Tricky]**

Manu: The painter paints the house.

Ravi: The carpenter digs the land.

Diya: The plumber builds the wall.

Sachin: The electrician fits wires, switches and bulbs.

Who among the four children made the correct statement?

(a) Manu and Sachin (b) Ravi only

(c) Diya and Sachin (d) Ravi and Diya

15. Study the given flow chart and select the correct option. **[Tricky]**

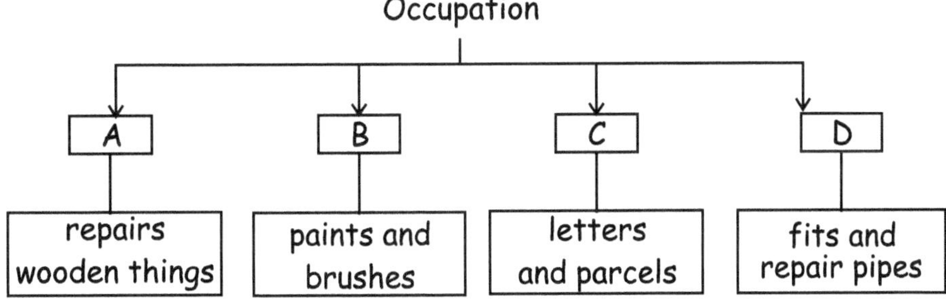

(a) A is a doctor and D is a plumber
(b) B is a painter, and C is a postman.
(c) C is a plumber.
(d) D is a carpenter.

16. Vineet: I need bread, butter, eggs, cup cakes, etc. [Tricky]
Sunny: I need medicines and some injection.
Where would Vineet and Sunny go to buy the things they need?

	Vineet	Sunny
(a)	Chemist	Hospital
(b)	Post office	Chemist
(c)	Stationery shop	Chemist
(d)	Grocery shop	Chemist

17. Select the correct match. [2013]

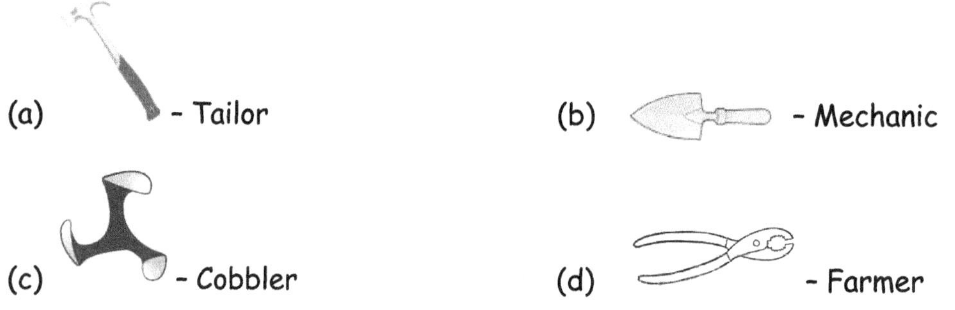

18. Fill up the missing alphabets to find out the correct occupation. [Tricky]

① O C ② ③ R

(a) D, T, E
(b) D, T, O
(c) E, T, D
(d) D, O, E

Directions (Qs. 19 to 22): Read the following passage carefully and answer the following question. [Critical Thinking]

There are many people who help us in our daily lives. The ability to do a task is known as skill. The work that help a person to earn a living is called occupation. There are many types of work that a person can do. Policeman protect us from thieves. A farmer grows crops to provide food to us. Carpenter make things of wood. A chemist sells medicines. We depend on all these people for our daily lives.

19. The work that helps a person to earn a living is called __________.

(a) job (b) skills

(c) occupation (d) All of these

20. Who provides food to us?

(a) Doctor (b) Chemist

(c) Farmer (d) Carpenter

21. Who protects us from thieves?

(a) Policeman (b) Traffic Police

(c) Farmer (d) None of these

22. Who makes our furniture?

(a) Carpenter (b) Policeman

(c) Chemist (d) Doctor

23. Match the Column (I) with Column (II) **[2014]**

Column I		**Column II**	
A.	Carpenter	1.	Space
B.	Farmer	2.	Shoes
C.	Astronaut	3.	Furniture
D.	Cobbler	4.	Grow crops & food

	A	B	C	D
(a)	1	2	3	4
(b)	3	2	4	1
(c)	3	4	1	2
(d)	2	3	4	1

24. Who grows crops, fruits and vegetables for us?

(a) Blacksmith (b) Mechanic (c) Farmer (d) Plumber

25. Read the following passage carefully and choose the correct answer.

1. Potter sends and receives messages from one place to another.

2. Tailor stiches our clothes. **[2015, Tricky]**

3. Carpenter catches thief.

(a) TTT (b) FFF (c) FTF (d) FTT

26. Who makes bread?

(a) Postman (b) Nurse (c) Baker (d) Teacher

27. Why it is necessary to respect each and every occupation? **[2016]**

(a) Because it gives us money.

(b) Each one of us needs the service of another.

(c) We depend on all these people for our daily needs.

(d) Both (b) and (c)

28. Which of the following among the childrens known as "Chacha Nehru".

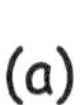
(a) 

M.S Dhoni

(b) 

Mahatma Gandhi

(c) 

Jawahar Lal Nehru

(d) 

Mother Teresa

29. Who sails the boat or ship? **[2017]**

(a) Carpenter. (b) Grocer (c) Sailor (d) Farmer

30. **Match the column (I) with column (II)** **[Tricky]**

Column I		Column II	
A.	Sachin Tendulkar	1.	Brings parcels and letters
B.	Jawahar Lal Nehru	2.	First Prime Minister of India
C.	Postman	3.	Put water on fire
D.	Fireman	4.	Cricketer

	A	B	C	D
(a)	1	2	3	4
(b)	4	3	2	1
(c)	4	2	1	3
(d)	3	2	1	4

RESPONSE GRID

LEVEL 1

1. a b c d	2. a b c d	3. a b c d	4. a b c d	5. a b c d
6. a b c d	7. a b c d	8. a b c d	9. a b c d	10. a b c d
11. a b c d	12. a b c d	13. a b c d	14. a b c d	15. a b c d
16. a b c d	17. a b c d	18. a b c d	19. a b c d	20. a b c d
21. a b c d	22. a b c d	23. a b c d	24. a b c d	25. a b c d
26. a b c d	27. a b c d			

LEVEL 2

1. a b c d	2. a b c d	3. a b c d	4. a b c d	5. a b c d
6. a b c d	7. a b c d	8. a b c d	9. a b c d	10. a b c d
11. a b c d	12. a b c d	13. a b c d	14. a b c d	15. a b c d
16. a b c d	17. a b c d	18. a b c d	19. a b c d	20. a b c d
21. a b c d	22. a b c d	23. a b c d	24. a b c d	25. a b c d
26. a b c d	27. a b c d	28. a b c d	29. a b c d	30. a b c d

Solutions with Explanation

LEVEL- 1

1. (c) Carpenter makes furniture at home.
2. (a) The man in the given figure is an astronaut.
3. (d) This is a potter and the missing alphabets are P O T T E R.
4. (c) Madhav is a cobbler.
5. (a) An engineer designs and builds road, metrorail, bridges etc.
6. (b) Sachin Tendulkar is the famous cricketer of India.
7. (d) All the others (Doctor, Nurse and Chemist) belong to medical profession.
8. (b) Plumber fits and repairs pipes at our home.
9. (b) This is Albert Einstein who works in the field of science.
10. (b) Jawahar Lal Nehru was the first Prime Minister of India.
11. (b) Mother Teresa was a social worker who helped poor, old and sick people.
12. (b) APJ Abdul Kalam was the famous scientist and the former President of India
13. (b) A waiter brings the dinner and bill in a restaurant.
14. (c) A mechanic can fix the problems related to car.
15. (c) A soldier works in army and carries gun.
16. (a) Tailor stiches our clothes.
17. (b) Nurse takes care of the sick people.
18. (b) Blacksmith makes and repair things made up of iron.
19. (c) A pilot flies the aeroplane.
20. (c)

21. (a) The first Indian to go into the space was Rakesh Sharma. Kalpana Chawala was the first Indian woman to visit space.

22. (c) Tailor stitches our clothes

23. (b) Kalpana Chawla was the first Indian women to go in the space.

24. (c) Plumber repairs taps and pipes.

25. (c) Neil Armstrong

26. (b)

27. (c)

LEVEL- 2

1. (d) The given image is a post-office. It help us to send message from one place to another and we buy letters and envelopes from here.

2. (c) A barber cut, trim and style our hairs.

3. (c) The person who sells the items shown in the given image is called **Grocer**.

4. (b) This is a nurse who takes care of the patient.

5. (c) Occupation

6. (a) Doctor

7. (b) Nurse

8. (c) postman

9. (b) blacksmith.

10. (b) wooden

11. (a) Doctor gives us medicine when we are sick.

12. (d) Mother teresa was a social worker and tailor stiches our clothes.

13. (d) 'X' is a chemist who sells medicines, 'Y' is APJ Abdul Kalam who was a scientist.

14. (a) Manu and Sachin made the correct statement.

The carpenter makes and repair wooden things. The plumber repairs and fits pipes.

15. (b) 'B' is a painter and 'C' is a postman.

16. (d) Vineet would go to Grocery shop to buy bread, butter, egg, cakes etc. and Sunny would go to a chemist to buy medicines.

17. (c) This tool is used by cobbler.

18. (b) This is a doctor and the missing alphabet are D O C T O R.

19. (c) occupation

20. (c) farmer

21. (a) policeman

22. (a) carpenter

23. (c) Carpenter makes furniture, farmer grows crops and food, astronaut go to space and cobbler repairs shoes.

24. (c) Farmer grows crops, fruit and vegetable for us.

25. (c) Postman send and receive messages and police catches thief.

26. (c) A baker makes the bread for us.

27. (d) We should respect each and every occupation because each one of us needs the service of another. We depend on all these people for our daily needs.

28. (c) Pandit Jawahar Lal Nehru is popular among the childrens as "Chacha Nehru".

29. (c) A sailor sails the boat or ship.

30. (c) Sachin Tendulkar is a cricketer, Jawahar Lal Nehru was the first Prime Minister of India, postman brings parcels and letter, fireman puts water on fire.

www.ingramcontent.com/pod-product-compliance
Lightning Source LLC
LaVergne TN
LVHW080459160826
845677LV00006B/1423
9789355644398